I DANCE WITH GOD

A COJOURNEY IN PRAYER

REV. CECELIA WILLIAMS BRYANT

Published by AKOSUA VISIONS

P.O. Box 41212
Dallas, Texas 75241

P.O. Box 39393
Baltimore, Maryland 21212

**I DANCE WITH GOD
A COJOURNEY IN PRAYER**

Copyright © 1995 by Cecelia Williams Bryant
All rights reserved

No part of this publication may be reproduced or transmitted in any form or by an means, electronic or mechanical, including photocopy, recording, or any information storage and retrieval system now known or to be invented, without written permission from the publisher.

Focus Scriptures are from the
New Revised Standard Version
of the Holy Bible (unless otherwise noted)
Copyright © 1989, by the Division of Christian Education
of the National Council of Churches of Christ
in the United States of America.
Oxford University Press • New York • 1989

All scripture quotations marked KJV are taken from
the King James Version of the Holy Bible

Hymns are from the AMEC Bicentennial Hymnal Published by the
African Methodist Episcopal Church • Nashville • 1984

COVER
Illustration by ARTIST—Kathleen Atkins Wilson
Title—"Rapture"
©1986

ISBN 1-888 077-01-8

AN OFFERING

I live my life as one who has been/is being
PRAYED FOR.

The Incessant Intercessions of
Mother Evelyn Simpson
Dr. Margaret Musgrove
Dr. Andrea Benton Rushing
ANNA DIGGS OKAI
CHARLOTTEE UMOJA
Cecelia Cameron

and the hidden host of praying daughers of NZINGA sustains
me on the journey. Because of their devotion and gentleness,
I am now able to make this OFFERING UNTO THE LORD

for the Blessing of Humanity,
the Healing of the Church,
the Reconciling of the Nations and

TO THE ETERNAL GLORY of GOD.

THE PATH

THE APOSTOLATE Dr. Ndugu T'Ofori Ata

NZINGA SPEAKS TO ME

   I. **"THIS IS *MY* BODY"**   1

"Then he took a loaf of bread, and when he had given thanks, he broke it and gave it to them, saying, "This is my body, which is given for you. Do this in remembrance of me." (Luke 22:19)

   II. **MOURNING INTO DANCING**   39

"You have turned my mourning into dancing; you have taken off my sackcloth and clothed me with joy," (Psalm 30:11)

   III. **SANKOFA BALLET**   64

"Do not remember the former things, or consider the things of old." (Isaiah 43:18)

   IV. **DANCE OF THE UNSPOKEN**   109

"When he is quiet, who can condemn? When he hides his face, who can behold him, whether it be a nation or an individual?" (Job 34:29)

   V. **THE INVISIBLE APOSTOLATE**   161

"Where then is my hope? Who will see my hope? Will it go down to the bars of Sheol? Shall we descend together into the dust?" (Job 17:15,16)

   VI. **COMMUNE WITH THINE HEART and BE STILL**   205

"Be still, and know that I am God! I am exalted among the nations, I am exalted in the earth." (Psalm 46:10)

"When you are disturbed, do not sin; ponder it on your beds, and be silent. Selah" (Psalm 4:4)

   VII. **THE GLORY AND THE DANCE AND THE GLORY**   243

"Then they will see 'the Son of Man coming in clouds' with great power and glory. Then he will send out the angels, and gather his elect from the four winds, from the ends of the earth to the ends of the heaven." (Mark 13:26,27)

"a time to weep, and a time to laugh; a time to mourn, and a time to dance;" (Ecclesiastes 3:4)

I DANCE WITH GOD—
A Cojourney in Prayer

Cecelia Williams Bryant, as in the order of the mystics, has been uniquely blessed with special, sensitive gifts of genetic spirituality. Her writings generate the kind of energetic expression as one in whom the hunger for God quickens deeper, and as one with an unquenchable thirst, profoundly driven by an a priori foretaste of Glory Divine.

These creative writings: in meditations, prose, poetry and psalm, with scriptural referencing, are probings of the spiritual cojourney in the life of prayer as dancing with God. In meditative quests for holiness, in prose profiling the soul in that dialectic of desire alternating between despair and hope, in poetry that illuminates the art and craft to put wings on wonderful words and holy conversations; in psalms that peak and peek with perceptions and visions from prayerful perspectives—wherein language stretches wide open the cojourners wings for high spiritual soaring. She is "dancing with God" in prayer. These are probings of the spirit to new heights in spheres, where the symphony of sounds, are prayers, unuttered or expressed, are sacred rhythms in the spiritual blending of the glory essence of music and meaning for dancing with God.

Cecelia opens to us an invitation to cojourney on seven pathways of prayer for experiencing in personal and corporate worship the intimate Divine-human encounter—in body, in mourning, in the past-future, in the unspoken, in the apostolate, in stillness, and in glory.

Dancing . . . as cojourneying in the life of prayer:

With a baring to nakedness, the body temple is presented and prostrated. In the struggles for disciplines of the spirit to be in faithful obedience and single-minded devotion to God, she incarnates the ritual of living dedication as the dance begins with the body in prostration, tingling with vibrations from the presence of Gods' tuning on the nerve fibers of the soul.

With a throbbing heart and a contrite spirit, she follows and leads in confessions about those deep bruises and hurts from the various afflictions in life that wound us and leave scars that bespeak the need for holy healing. The written ritual guides us into the mourning cartharsis wherein the spirit of God releases us from the captivities of fear and rejection, humiliation and hate. All of the conspiracies of negative forces are cast into the "streams of holiness from the River of God."

With flowing intensity of precious and lingering memories, coursing in consciousness, she writes as one within form and informed, shaped under possession of the Holy Other. In this prayer-spell, she is dancing with gliding instructions of the Will of God and with inspiration from the Word of God, "Centered in the flow of the Breath of God."

With flickering affirmations in hopes when human hope unborn would have died unspoken, yet she, beholding to be firm and holding fast to the undying holy fire of spiritual hope, radiates like a dazzling diamond. In language aglow and prayer lights bursting from the flash of those inner lights turned on by the Light of life and power of spirit, God is dancing so softly and silently releasing redeeming, regenerating and healing forces of salvation reflections of dancing around Calvary—affirming that awesome drama of Redemption as God's dancing partner and having given Jesus, the unspoken now spoken, resurrection order that Hope is Eternal, and Jesus came "dancing out of the tomb."

With daring imagination, the apostolate had accepted the invitation to dance with God, reverential moments are timeless in praising with unceasing adoration in every experience claiming every moment the opportunity for the unconditional yes to the sweet invitation to receive the Holy Spirit depositing for us all a touch of glory. In a word she shouts Glory, "God has come to dance with me."

With breathing eternity into the breast, an inward peace comes from dancing as cojourner in prayer obedience. Our focus is now on the flowing in of that life-force God has ordained when no word need be spoken and the experience of the Supernatural is in the dancing stillness. Such calming serenity awaits those who are yielding to dancing like waves beckoning invitation to all who would enter the dance of still living waters where deep is calling to partnering with deep. Come dance in the Ocean of God's Love. Let the Dance begin: "Prayer is leaping off the diving board of invocation into the Ocean of God."

Dr. Ndugu T'Ofori Ata

NZINGA SPEAKS TO ME

To Pray is to Dance is to Pray
      is to Worship
      is to Resist
      is to Commune
      is to Liberate
      is to Reveal
      is to Reverence
      is to Wait
      is to Rise
      is to Honor
      is to Yield
      is to Sanctify
      is to Listen
      is to Pray
      is to Dance
      is to Pray
To the ALMIGHTY GOD!

    What you are about to encounter is the raw data of an African-ancestored woman's pursuit of Holiness. I take you there not as a matter of due course, but rather in compelling obedience to the Resurrected Reality of JESUS Christ. I am not a witness to some nameless, anonymous deity. I aspire to live to the praise of His Glory. I invite you there with the expectation that you, by the Power of the Holy Ghost will sort through the desiderata of my mortal anguish and touch God. It is as formidable an assignment as that of Queen Nzinga who attempted to organize Angolan resistance to the Portugese slave traders in the 1600's.

    Know This. PRAYER is RESISTANCE. PRAYER is an ACT of Defiance. It is a revolutionary weapon of the highest magnitude. To pray is to establish Solidarity in the Supernatural Realm. The terror of Evil is a Life of Prayer! Now we know. Now we make our departures from the corrosive delusion of "historical" facticity and enter that intangible hemisphere identified simply as the **HOPE** of the oppressed.

NZINGA 2

"He removed the high places . . . . for until those days the children of Israel burned incense to it, and called it Nehushtan."

(II Kings 18:4)

The praying Apostolate surpasses every other calling in intensity
    PURPOSE
  breadth
    GRACE
    VISION
and LIGHT.

The Call to Prayer is an invitation to DIE. Who can enter the Presence of GOD and Live? Nor should one desire to do so. The Call to PRAYER is the gateway to the CHRIST nature. It is the chamber of preparation for the Messianic mind. Rituals are safer. Highly preferable to an undisclosed Life of indeterminate Spirituality. LOGOS, eros, Pathos—each is taken to its fullest dimension in surrendered Prayer. Prayer that is inward, rhapsodic, centered, and washed in DIVINITY. This praying not only transforms lives; but awakens Destiny.

THE DANCE is begun. The oppressed return to the altar of the LIVING GOD. The "high places" of their accusers are abandoned. We "shake the dust from our feet." We hear the buried tapping the lids of their coffins. This Dance will end with Resurrection. RESISTANCE NEVER DIES.

"I am THE LORD'S   I am African   I am Woman
*   Diaspora sorrows have filled the cup from which I have had to drink. I am my sister's sister. From Guyana, South America, Haiti, Trinidad, the Virgin Islands, Barbados, the Cayman Islands, Bermuda, Jamaica; I perceive our resilient HOPE. NIGERIA, GHANA, The GAMBIA, SIERRA LEONE, COTE D'IVOIRE, LIBERIA, SENEGAL and GABON remind me to honor the beauty of the moment. NAMIBIA, SWAZILAND and SOUTH AFRICA have inspired me with the INTEGRITY of our STRUGGLE. Jordan and Israel press me to PRAY through to the mystery. France, London, Australia, Canada and the United States compel me to know myself, Respect my People and HONOR my vows. My husband, John, has been my covering—in prayer, in the throes of Spiritual Warfare; in the controversies of the institutional Church; in the parenting of our Blessings: Jamal Harrison and Thema Simone. Pauline Lucas Williams, my mother, is my perpetual Intercessor and my Friend."*

Cecelia Williams Bryant

THIS IS MY BODY

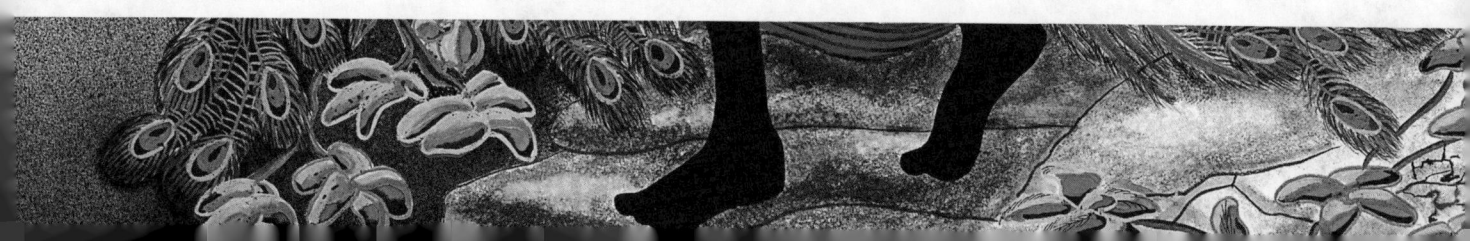

The Healing Work of the SPIRIT of GOD defies all natural "laws" and consideration. Let us from the outset NAME those issues in the world, the Church, the Culture and our lives that MUST be Healed! As we continue our journey together, we Shall prevail in prayer concerning each one:

-
-
-
-
-
-
-
-
-
-
-
-
-
-
-
-
-
-
-
-
-
-
-
-
-
-
-
-
-
-
-

ONE

"Then the LORD replied with gracious and comforting words to the angel who talked with me." (Zechariah 1:13)

The seed of the oppressed carry *within our bodies* the prayers and longings of those who "have gone the way of all the earth." (1 Kings 2:2) *In our bodies* we remember and know things. See things. Experience realities far *before* and *beyond* the present day. Our muted prayings consist in two words—"How Long?" "How Long?"

The Spirit of the Lord has answered me saying "It will not be as long as it has been!" This is the refreshing. The words of the Lord. This is the refreshing. And so we must prepare ourselves for a new world reality. A more true Vision of God. A clear self understanding. A discernment of the Hope for the future of the world. Is it so incredible to consider that this is the fruit of PRAYER? That only prayer has the power to so transform the human spirit and personality so completely; with such spiritual grace, that the nations themselves will ultimately be regenerated! That total prayer—Soul, Intellect, Passion, and Body—is the unique reality of a life surrendered to GOD! This is the mark of the Visionary. The Apostle. The LIGHT—bringer. She to whom the word is spoken: "The Glory of the Lord rises upon you." (Isaiah 60:1)

She lives to pray.
She prays to see.
She sees to heal.
She heals to change.
She changes to FREE.
SHE FREES TO PRAY.

I DANCE WITH GOD

A worldly spirituality is not intimidated by Violence. Violence is the soulless manifestation of rage. It is domestic, theological, global and personal. As a "GUIDE" receiving "GUIDANCE," I am praying that our collaboration in PRAYER will unleash a torrent of Healings in the Universe.

ONE

"You have made your people suffer hard things; you have given us wine to drink that made us reel."

(Psalm 60:3)

"Why do the wicked renounce God, and say in their hearts, "You will not call us to account? But you do see! Indeed you note trouble and grief, that you may take it into your hands; the helpless commit themselves to you; you have been the helper of the orphan."

(Psalm 10:13,14)

"And this is eternal life, that they may know you, the only true God, and Jesus Christ whom you have sent."

(John 17:3)

"But we do not want you to be uninformed, brothers and sisters, about those who have died, so that you may not grieve as others do who have no hope. For since we believe that Jesus died and rose again, even so, through Jesus, God will bring with him those who have died."

(1 Thessalonians 4:13,14)

"For the Lord himself, with a cry of command, with the archangel's call and with the sound of God's trumpet, will descend from heaven, and the dead in Christ will rise first. Then we who are alive, who are left, will be caught up in the clouds together with them to meet the Lord in the air; and so we will be with the Lord forever. Therefore encourage one another with these words."

(1 Thessalonians 4:16–18)

Today, I am immensely challenged by the undeterred presence of EVIL
in the world
in the church
in the human condition. Herein lies the cosmic paradox: Generations of prophets and poets, seers and healers, dancers and magicians have journeyed across the planet harboring in their bosoms the Light of an eternal and fluorescent Beauty. This LIGHT is for humanity the only source of LIFE.

Yet our fascination with evil. Our coarse irreverence. Our contempt for simplicity and utter disregard for the sacred. These things have obstructed our vision of the path. More especially, our fear of SILENCE.

Prayer is the sole path to the LIGHT, of which I am certain! To know GOD is the whole dignity of CREATION. To know oneSelf as LIGHT-bringer (Nukukhanye)* is to penetrate evil. To perfect BEAUTY. To resist and hold back the deluge of oppression. To thwart the enemy.

"The Spirit of the LORD is encamped about us." Even when the deluge afflicts humanity with blindness and piercing egoism. It seems at that moment that there is no music. Worst of all, the deluge warps the heart songs of the innocent. Fierce and agonizing hopelessness is the fruit of the deluge. Who can escape?

The world.

The church.

And the human condition.

Each seeks to accommodate the deluge with the expectation of some sort of reprieve. There is NONE. Only TERROR. Death is not enough. It does not satisfy. There must be TERROR of the first magnitude. The infirmities of our minds and bodies are so much stored up terror! The debris of TERROR.

Send for the LIGHT BRINGERS. Send for those who will not be overcome by the TERROR. Send for those who are not ashamed of death. Send for those who can still hear the music. Send for those who can swim against the Deluge! These are the women who have been found by God and Know God. Amen.

---

*A word spoken by the Zulu of South Africa

ONE

How can we know them? Have they an emblem, a badge, a sound? You will see the sign. It's in the movement of our bodies. The swift gestures of our hands. The sullen posture of our lips. The erect anchor of our backs. The width of our toes. The fire in our eyes. Our rounded bellies. The rings around our necks. The heaving of our bosoms, GOD is not DEAD. Once you see us, there is no time to escape. No cellar to flee to. No village of refuge. We are God's answer to God's question: "Who will go for us?" (Isaiah 6:8)

Our tears are our HOPE
                our memory
                our warfare
                our PRAYERS.

Search our bodies and you will find the clue to TERROR Resistance. We give ourselves to GOD *in our bodies*.
    to our men *in our bodies*
    to our children *in our bodies*
    to the world *in our bodies*
    to Destiny *in our bodies*.

For a moment, religion taught us to condemn our bodies. Divorce them. Cover them. Resist them. Repent for them. Store up shame in them. The subtlety of the Deluge: render woman too psychologically insecure, unstable, TERRIFIED—to know/love her own Body. Shame and Hopelessness and reification were the triune buriel ground of this black glory. But when we saw into the Spirit world the reflected LIGHT of a Greater Beauty, we took possession of our bodies again. Again. Again. Unsure, but trying.
Not understanding. But trying.
Closing our eyes at FIRST. But trying.

The Holy SPIRIT of GOD is teaching us to HEAL and EXIT our wounded places. The HOLY SPIRIT, GOD is teaching us to LISTEN to our BODY wisdom and understand life's mysteries. Our bodies make welcome the Spirit in our devotions.

> *"Take good care to observe the commandment and instruction that Moses the servant of the LORD commanded you, to love the LORD your God, to walk in all his ways, to keep his commandments, and to hold fast to him, and to serve him with all your heart and with all your soul."*
>
> (Joshua 22:5)

ONE

"Those who are wise shall shine like the brightness of the sky, and those who lead many to righteousness, like the stars forever and ever."

(Daniel 12:3)

God is not offended
  by these hips
      these legs
      this hair
      these shoulders.

Let the icons of the culture be smashed against the wall of commercialism. There is LIGHT in me for the world.

"Let it SHINE.
 Let it Shine.
 Let it Shine,"

I begin as I welcome my body to the Universe—every part. Promising. "I will not be ashamed anymore." Not as a cheap superficial gimmick. Rather at a depth level to remember myself in the HOLY Ghost as I RE-member myself in the POWER of Creation in the Name of JESUS. Motion comes easy. Because to pray is to be carried.

To be Moved.

To Pass Over.

To Enter in.

To launch out.

To leap.

To genuflect unto completion.

To Commune.

To communicate.

To touch.

To experience.

To be made ALIVE.

    To PRAY, (To Dance), is to be God's Darling. Sweet fruit. (I have been heading in this direction ever since *before*.) I cannot make myself "ready." I know the very enterprise of resistance. It begins with a Biblically grounded affirmation:

        "THE LORD IS WITH ME."

"With GOD, nothing shall be impossible."

(Luke 1:37)

There is no situation in which I find myself that the LORD is <u>NOT</u> WITH Me. I am VICTORIOUS ONLY because THE LORD IS WITH ME.

"THIS IS MY BODY" • 5

ONE

I speak to myself THIS REALITY: "THE LORD IS WITH ME."
I contend with the adversary from this power base:

"THE LORD IS WITH ME."

This turbulence is NOT MINE to conquer. It is the LORD's.
This sickness is NOT MINE to heal. It is THE LORD's.
This VISION is NOT MINE to manifest. It is THE LORD's.

THE LORD IS WITH ME.

The enterprise of RESISTANCE is at the OUTSET an interior movement. I must take to heart the scriptural teaching—"Without Faith, it is impossible to please GOD." (Heb. 11:6) The life of the oblate *must* be a life of FAITH.
> Undistracted Faith.
> LOVING Faith.
> Innocent Faith.

With this FAITH, I pray to be centered in the *ACTIVE* awareness of the LOVE of GOD.

For I am Healed by LOVE. Amazed by LOVE. "Conquered by LOVE." To LIVE in GOD's LOVE, is to live WISELY. To live in GOD's LOVE is to receive every gracious expression of LOVE. To live in GOD's LOVE, is to respond to the beauty in the world. In LOVE, I acknowledge the Vision. The vision needs LIGHT. LIFE. AIR. Affirmation. ME. This is the power of RESISTANCE.

ONE

"Fear not . . ."

    (Daniel 10:19)

    (John 12:15)

    (Luke 1:13)

    (Isaiah 7:4)

    (Isaiah 54:4)

    (Joel 2:21)

    (Matthew 10:28)

In the midst of the deluge I PRAY:

"Holy Jesus,
cause me to *experience*
Your DIVINE LOVE—
Blessing me . . .
Protecting me . . .
Healing me . . .
Saving me . . ."

I continue in PRAYER until the prayer itself consumes and transforms my Reality.
And then I Bless the NAME of the LORD.
    With my whole heart.
    And with my mouth.
    And in my thoughts.
    And with my body.
    And with my gifts.
    And with my TITHES.
    And with my OFFERINGS.
RESISTANCE must be ABSOLUTE.
            UNCOMPROMISED.
    Lacking ulterior MOTIVATION.
        PURE.
Only then does it qualify as a Godly enterprise.

And now that there is nothing more to tolerate or abandon, I give myself. It is not the obedience of Despair. The whisper of melancholy. The vital sign of desperation. It is the genuine response of a liberated Soul. One who is not the possession of society, the denomination or the clan. I have no home in religion. No comraderie among the "approved." No ambition for the culture. Now that I am naked, I will Dance/PRAY forever. Because, like Job's, "my Prayer is Pure." (Job 16:17)

ONE

The enterprise of RESISTANCE is continuous. Because the press to conform is persistant. The temptation to compromise is subtle. The weaknesses of the flesh innumerable. If, indeed you are "called" to be a Cojourner, you must discipline your MIND, your BODY and your SPIRIT to RESIST.

Let Us pray to the LORD—

Holy FIRE,
Sacred flame,
Eternal LIGHT . . .
Burn in me.
Burn away the dross of
    pettiness,
    indulgence,
    procrastination,
    and superficility.
Set me ablaze with
    Courage.
    Tenacity.
    and Sanctified IMAGINATION!
in the NAME of JESUS.

    Amen.

ONE

The "LIGHT BRINGERS" are praying Souls. Those for whom PRAYER is spontaneous. Unhindered. OPEN. The Soul advanced in PRAYER is the "true believer." Prayer is a FORTRESS
>> a BRIDGE and
>> A RIVER of GOD.

Prayer is the inflow of the Sacred.
The reluctance to pray—genuine PRAYER—has dissipated the Church and allowed chaos to permeate the world. The "religious" are like Adam and Eve in the garden HIDING FROM GOD!
"We need PRAYER." This is the name of the ministry of Rev. Marie Antoinette Phillips of Baltimore, Maryland. And it continues to be true! WE NEED PRAYER.
> To rediscover the LOVE of GOD.
> To experience the breadth and dignity of Creation.
> To restore the INTEGRITY of the Church.
> To raise up a NEW GENERATION of HOPE.
> To heal the NATIONS. And
> To find our way to each other!

Prayer draws the Soul to the highest plane of enlightenment. Prayer leaps over the barriers of reason and opens the windows of the Spirit. Prayer incarnates GOD. The "word is made flesh." Mortality is transfigured. Prayer actualizes the descent of Divinity.

ONE

Why should a Soul in need of LOVE try to hide from GOD?
Why should a woman whose bowels have burst open flee from the One who makes whole?
Why should one who has slept with the scent of death in her nostrils reject the offer of Life?
So "Let US PRAY."
    Let us PRAY until torment dematerializes.
        Let us PRAY until the wicked are awakened at midnight by
            visions of the Souls they have offended.
        Let us PRAY until we no longer fear to HOPE.
        Let us PRAY into new formations of solidarity.
        Let us PRAY into a gracious
            disregard of Rejection.
        Let us PRAY TO ASCEND,
            TO TRANSFORM.
            TO Heal.
            TO See God.

Such Praying will of course alienate the Oblate from every false sense of self. Such praying will quicken an inner duality such that our pre-covenant self and our covenanting Soul can be found dialoguing, struggling and dancing with each other.

By sanctification, our pre-covenant Soul-life diminishes and singularity of vision, purpose and Hope emerge.

The following is a rather circuitous parable of sorts. A didactic, if you will. A meandering. An apocalyptic exposé—in a manner of speaking. Pray to hear. Embrace the struggle. Flow with the meaning. Give yourself permission to laugh, to weep, to cry out! To breathe.

ONE

"Therefore keep the commandments of the LORD your God, by walking in his ways and by fearing him. For the LORD your God is bringing you into a good land, a land with flowing streams, with springs and underground waters welling up in valleys and hills, a land of wheat and barley, of vines and fig trees and pomegranates, a land of olive trees and honey."

(Deuteronomy 8:6–8)

"My anguish, my anguish! I writhe in pain! Oh, the walls of my heart! My heart is beating wildly; I cannot keep silent; for I hear the sound of the trumpet, the alarm of war. Disaster overtakes disaster, the whole land is laid waste. Suddenly my tents are destroyed, my curtains in a moment. How long must I see the standard, and hear the sound of the trumpet? For my people are foolish, they do not know me; they are stupid children, they have no understanding. They are skilled in doing evil, but do not know how to do good."

(Jeremiah 4:19–22)

A RHYTHM FOR LIVING.

Chords of LOVE and Holiness reverberate in my soul like the tremor on the platform of an approaching subway. The mounting intensity draws me to the threshold of Belonging.

The moment you arrive; you know you are *there*. Having lived so much of my life feeling   dis-situated
>> out-of-sorts
>> dis-placed
>> un-centered.

I now know what it means to be at home.
> ONE.
> Welcomed.
> IN-FLOW.

From time to time, I could glimpse this moment in the fires
of poetic passion
or ecstatic Prayer
or the burst of orange at sunset
or the artistic momentum of a grieving harp.
I never dreamed that someday or midnight I would actively, actually LIVE here. Here where I BELONG.
Without the anxiety of offending.
Without the delusion of acceptance.
Without the tribe of mediocrity.
> To BELONG to GOD and oneSelf—

What risks am I willing to take?
What/who am I willing to give up?

BELONGING is fuschia—silk fuschia and a peridot stone. BELONGING is looking out the window of a skyscraper, seeing the city, and *knowing* that the prayers of your heart far surpass all the riches therein. BELONGING is the wilderness *and* The Promised Land.

ONE

I am not LOST. I am at Home. This is the place that PRIESTS and POETS, Prophets and Dancers meet GOD and reach for the sky!
It is no longer a lonely place. (They stopped calling months ago. Maybe years.) As I pass into a network of solace, I remember the mood of Paradise when last I entered the threshold of Belonging. It is a tedious journey. Travelling from the myth of self to the REALITY of Being HOLY. The monastic life is one of vegetation, wind, Light and drums. Periodically a swan, a dove, (never an ostrich!) or even a humming bird. But most of all MUSIC and COLOR. The mystery of Life is the persistance of BEAUTY. The HONOR of Simplicity. The miracle of Hope. To pray, woman must lay down Death. She must stop circling the universe of despair and live within Her own Soul meaning. God cannot be shaken. (Unless, of course, it is God's decision.)
I have learned that Morning does not begin with the sun nor Midnight with the moon. "The fullness of time" happens! There is rarely a measurable sequence of learnings. It is a matter of the Biblical "suddenly." This was when I allowed mySelf to know the great emptiness that is in the heart of all manner of believers. (Most especially my own!)

"Vanity of vanities,
says the Teacher,
vanity of vanities!
All is vanity." (Ecclesiastes 1:2)

Dear Cojourner,
    Have you filled your thoughts,
              your days,
              your life,
              with emptiness? . . .

ONE

"If you belonged to the world, the world would love you as its own. Because you do not belong to the world, but I have chosen you out of the world—therefore the world hates you."

(John 15:19)

I am learning to bow gracefully (GRATEFULLY) out of the priorities of others.
I am learning to taste the Rain that falls on my own lips,
    Hear the echo of Promises made to
        my Self that remain unkept;
    Sense the meaning in the shadows
        that dance through the RIVER of my thoughts;
    Tarry at the Altar, Lying on my back,
        staring in the Dark at the ceiling until it moves!

Suddenly.
Morning comes.
Suddenly
There is midnight after all.
I have entered the threshold of my BELONGING. All my life, I have been trying to get here. Even when I knew it not. Even when I fought the wind. Even when I entered the house of death. Even when I became insane. I was on my way here. I am learning that if I write long enough, I will write myself into
WELLNESS,
Companionship,
Rain Forests and
the
Galaxy.

Because prayer has taken possession of my pen; And my pen has become a willing servant of prayer, NOW my SOUL has an instrument with which to talk to GOD, interpret GOD and give expression to the Unknown. When I go where I BELONG, I find that GOD is there already!

                              SELAH.

ONE

Tommorow will Come.
SUDDENLY.   And when it does, MAY I be found a TRUE oblation unto the Lord.

What Prayer of the heart will quicken the Joy of the Kingdom?
How can we PRAY such that we render ourselves of no consequence and completely surrender volition
    in the Praying moment?
Have we not rendered our prayers in *vanity*?
What is our *BODY LANGUAGE* when we pray?
LET the Soul desiring to advance in prayer contemplate these things **IN RETREAT**. So as to astonish the spirit of pride. So as to expose the indulgence of *personality*. And ultimately to purify our desire.
        Temper us with humility.
        Open us to our true vocation.
    and establish us in the Vision of GOD.
        WHERE WE BELONG.

> "Teach me Your way, O Lord;
> I will walk in Your truth;
> Unite my heart to fear Your
> name."   (Psalm 86:11 NK3V)

I am learning that spirituality is no mean thing. It is NOT, as some suppose, INTELLECTUALISM. Nor, to the dismay of others, is it EMOTIONALISM. The SPIRIT is greater than both. DEEPER. PURE. Perfect. GOD is SPIRIT. The SPIRIT is GOD. The whole of life is the journey of the Soul to ONEness with GOD.

ONE

THE ENCHANTED LIFE OF OBLATION

Why would mere mortals give up wealth and fame?
Flee the comforts of *civilation*?
Choose Celibacy?
Endure isolation?
Spend *days* without eating?
Give money to *strangers*?
Live in *foreign* cultures?
Submit to authority?
Give up their vacation time?
Dwell with the forgotten?
Give their lives for those who *hate* them?

There is a REASON. It is to BE ONE with the LORD. Somehow, the power of this reality cannot be adequately languaged. You must *EXPERIENCE* THE CALL! Every impulse of Your Soul Life must be energized by the LOVE of GOD. Somehow in your heart you become readily, receptively *OPEN* to the PRESENCE of GOD. Your entire being is supernaturally *divinized*. You are thrust into the natural order as a Spiritual Eminence! Even the countenance of the Oblate is ablaze with the Light of the LOVE of GOD. You are *drawn, driven* and *directed* by a hallowed INNER fire.

The Oblate knows that the POWER
the FORCE
the ENERGY
is GOD.

The Oblate is FREE **ONLY** when she is living in the GIFT. Oblation is the Self-Offering of the Soul advanced in Prayer. It is the manifested reality of a prevailing Cojourner. Oblation is finding fullness in empty places. It is walking toward a closed door *expecting* it to open. OBLATION is CHRIST. Oblation is authentically CHRIST.

Do you want to know what creates OBLATION?
Desire.
Suffering.
Generosity.
Music.
Gentleness
Forgiveness
Courage.
Eccentricity.
PRAYER.
Solitude.
Communion.
Discipline.

DESIRE

The Oblate life is one of Passionate Devotion. One cannot be under the curse of Ephesus—"neither hot nor cold." (Rev. 3:15) It is to feel deeply. Allowing the Holy Spirit to burrow through all other desires and longings. So that I may draw in God. Supernaturally High.

DESIRE is one of the mysteries of the inner life. How is it conceived? Nurtured? What causes it's demise? The life and death of desire has been the fare of poets and musicians since GOD said "LET" . . . and there IS! There are persons who are possessed of this DESIRE at birth. The rest of us must earnestly pray for it.

    Wrestle with angels!
    Prevail through fasting.

And even with all this; yet we must WAIT without flaunting our intentions. Um m m. Every other desire pales in comparison.

Continually Let us Pray to the LORD . . .

    "Holiness,
      impart to me
      the desire to
      DESIRE you
      ONLY.
      COMPLETELY.
      FREELY."
          Amen

ONE

"But as for me, I will look to the LORD, I will wait for the God of my salvation; my God will hear me. Do not rejoice over me, O my enemy; when I fall, I shall rise; when I sit in darkness, the LORD will be, a light to me."

(Micah 7:7,8)

I

ONE

"If we live, we live to the Lord, and if we die, we die to the Lord; so then, whether we live or whether we die, we are the Lord's."

(Romans 14:8)

III

"Whoever is kind to the poor lends to the LORD, and will be repaid in full."

(Proverbs 19:17)

II

SUFFERING

In pain was I born. In pain will I be buried. The world is so much with me. In me. I lapse into comas of powerlessness when I "burn out" because of overload and expectation. "Surely He has borne my grief, carried my sorrows." (Isaiah 53:4) I remember. And I die and LIVE again. This time Belonging. Amen.

Martyrdom is not in the dying. Martyrdom is in the LIVING. What is new is not the suffering; but the will to LIVE in the POWER of the GIFT—ANYHOW! The Pain calls us back to the GIFT. Suffering arouses the PROMISE of the GIFT. Difficulty is no longer intimidating. The symptoms of menopause are powerless in the life of the Soul advanced in Prayer. SPIRIT PREVAILS. AMEN

GENEROSITY

The woman who believes she has nothing to give. Refuses to Give. Finds Giving offensive. Has no room for God. I am learning to give without consideration of the outcome. "Secret alms." (Matthew 6:1) Giving without the legitimacy of occasion. GIVING to enemies, strangers, children and women in far away places. Not to be LOVED.

Justified.
Forgiven.

"Lending" to the Lord. Amen.

Generosity is a Spiritual grace. It is GOD pouring out blessings to the world through an open channel—the heart of the Oblate. Generosity is the insignia of a praying heart. To GIVE your time
your resources
your interest
yourSELF. GIVEN FREELY.
LOVINGLY. Spontaneously. Joyfully. THIS IS CHRIST.
This is CHRIST.
Amen.

MUSIC
What is Music to the Deaf? It is a move of the Soul. It is the Fire of adoration. The rhythm of Cosmic impulse energizing HOPE. This Music can *only* be heard in the SILENCE. Stringed instruments. We who are the Zeze of God. Played by the Spirit, Drawn by the Power. A decibal beyond hurt. This is the JOY unspeakable! The WELL without bottom. Beyond height and breadth and width and depth. Intense. Incredible Illumined. There is SONG in this. Eternal under the stars! Amen.

GENTLENESS
Tenderness, Gentleness, Kindness, Sweetness, Innocence. All resistance purged, EASY with my Self, OTHERS. Easy with GOD. A radical departure from New York cynicism, skepticism. Hot ice. Loss of necessity for brash and those who are! "The fiery darts of the enemy are quenched." (Ephesians 6:16) Amen.

FOREGIVENESS
The pillars of my Cathedral of Oblation will crumble under the weight of UNFORGIVENESS. Somehow, listening to the wind, the waters, the future; I understand that the offender need not merit, deserve or even seek forgiveness. Conferring it does something liberating in me! A channel of Divinity is opened that would otherwise remain locked. Because I am not hostage to the injury, I am infused by the RADIANCE of Divine Glory. I drink deep of the stream of Benedictions that flow from the throne of GOD. Amen.

COURAGE
    True FAITH gives birth to the Courage to face mySelf. Be MYSELF. LOVE MYSELF. Live within the REALITY of me. This must be Paradise! I Belong Here. Autumn in my mind. Colorful transformations. Less day. More night. Sweet blue blackness. Halo over the Moon. No need to Run. Come gently home to the hemisphere of my Belonging. I can change the temperature around the world. dEVIL works will be stopped by this invisible FORCE: Holiness. The inner strength to emotionally triumph over the assult of relationships. GOD is not Afraid! Amen.

IV

V

VI

VII

ONE

"including yourselves who are called to belong to Jesus Christ,"

(Romans 1:6)

ONE

VIII ECCENTRICITY

Sameness does not breathe. Has no passion. No Risk. No REAL Dignity. Whether Hoodlum or Mainstream; sameness is awkward, tentative, corrupting. Unremembered. Quickly forgotten. Rarely mentioned. Dismissed. Eccentricity sets the artist FREE. No one expects the ARTIST/Prophet to Conform. To be assimilated. To adhere to the stereotype. That is why God could Speak Himself out of Cosmic non-BEING. This is the Wonder, within which I am imaged—TRINITY: Creator, REDEEMER, HEALER. Three natures in One. This is true LOVE. Unseparated. Unregimented. ONE. Completion. Ever Always Being. I Belong Here. Amen.

IX PRAYER

I Stop taking spirits to bed with me who do not understand LOVE. Their progeny are always ugly. And so I "PRAY without Ceasing." (1 Thessalonians 5:17) LOVE without End. Undistracted by personality (at last!) PRAYER is life. IT is the way in which God and I are able to touch each other. Even when reduced to wordless desire; as a patient in the Intensive Care Unit. Prayer Hopes. Authentic Prayer is a continuous LOVE Dance. Amen.

"Innocence" prepares the heart for prayer. "Innocence" opens our lives to the knowledge of GOD. Pray with the heart of a child—harmless, "UNSOPHISTICATED," honest. PRAY into an "awareness" of the PRESENCE of GOD. PRAY in OPEN-NESS to the SPIRIT. Pray *Knowing* that you are LOVED. Heard. Included.

When you PRAY to be FORGIVEN; BELIEVE that you are. Let this faith bring you Healing and Freedom. Then RISE up FORGIVE and bless others. And so shall we Heal the WORLD, the Church, the family and our own wounded hearts.

SOLITUDE

Most of all, OBLATION is Solitude. No spouse. No children. No relations. God is the center of my universe. A lone barren tree in this wilderness of Sorrow until the tears of Jesus wash over me. I learn to fight back for myself. To believe in the virtue of my own consent. To draw back from remedial assimilationist—approval oriented actions.

Invocations are in tongues. And tears. And Trembling. Music calls me to mySelf. "JESUS," I say, believe, think, breathe, hear. "JESUS."

His Presence exposes the shame, guilt, resentment that are just beneath the surface of my Hope. "JESUS" waits for me to walk out to Him. Alone Without crutches. Crawl. Determined to reach Him. Alone. The nutrition of Solitude is confidence in God and learning to LOVE and CHERISH me! (Why would I offer Abba that which I reject?) Selah.

X   ONE

COMMUNION

I joy in having someone to pray with. In speaking the NAME together. In laying in the darkness together to listen to the SILENCE together. We gather to play with the Angels. To Dance before the Host of Heaven. To laugh with God. I am united by the breath of God with the Souls of the Dead and the Visions of the unborn. We draw strength to Heal the Nations. Call down Fire. Call down cleansing Fire. Hope is burning in the hearts of the Nations. I touch the Earth with my prayers. The earth touches me. We are no longer Afraid to know one another. So it is with the waters, the mountains, and the Trees. God alive in US. Forever. Amen.

IX

ONE   XII

"For all of us must appear before the judgment seat of Christ, so that each may receive recompense for what has been done in the body, whether good or evil."

(2 Corinthians 5:10)

DISCIPLINE

PURPOSE is a jealous LOVER. "All things cohere" in it. By it, I am born anew. PURPOSE is Fresh Water on dry ground. PURPOSE calls to me and I answer. The matter of Discipline is an intriguing one. I am *learning* that it is something *beyond* compulsion. (Which by its very nature is sick and inflexible.) Discipline that flows from LOVE consciousness is the Journey. It is awakened by a compelling desire for GOD. It is an unregimented CONSISTENCY in responding to the Presence of God in the world

    in the WORD
    in Solitude
    in Community
    in Worship
    in Work
    in Meditation
    in Vision
    in Waiting.

It is releasing all the attributes of Death and spontaneously celebrating the Sanctity of Life in all persons

                      and situations
                      and creatures
                      and planets.

This I am seeking to know and believe. I have learned that of the two PURPOSE is the mother and discipline the daughter.

PURPOSE
births
nurtures
instructs
LOVES, counsels, chastises and
celebrates DISCIPLINE. **Selah**.

These 12 glimpses into the life of Oblation are Not exhaustive. Yet, surely if one flows in anyone of them long enough, deeply enough; you will be carried to the source—GOD. What is intriguing is the unique way in which our bodies resonate with the POWER from the *SOURCE* whenever we are given over in prayer to "THE CALL." Oblation is an opportunity for perfection in a broken world. It is the icon of BEAUTY, SIMPLICITY and Redemption.

ONE

Sweet, sweet OBLATION washes the scales from my eyes. Gives me sight. Cures my blindness. And I can SEE the "Glory of the Lord Rising upon" me! It takes some getting used to. It takes exhaling the string of rejections brooding over my Soul. It takes listening to LOVE songs ALONE after dark. It takes waking up in the arms of angels. It takes reading a REAL love letter and listening to my heart weep for hours. Weep and moan. Moan and grieve. Cry and hurt. Because I am so far away. It takes smelling the incense two days after the fire has gone out. It takes waiting for the tornado to come. It takes torrential rain. It takes GOD.
    Always God.
    Only God.
This IS a flash-flood watch!
                          Amen.

It is not long before the Oblate begins to reclaim the sanctity of her body.
    A new body consciousness speaks healing affirmations:
My BODY is a Gift of GOD.
My BODY is the Sanctuary of my Divine Purpose.
My BODY is an expression of the mystery of GOD.
Every cell in my BODY houses a memory of GOD's LOVE for ME.
The rhythm of Eternity flows in my Body.
    DAILY, affirmations are born in the Life of the Oblate. In the absence of PRAYER, Life does not exist. There is no Reality. Separation from GOD is death. Non-being. PRAYER is LIFE. The marginalized, the forgotten, the POOR, the anonymous—We must heighten our PRAYINGS in order to transform the emptiness created by those who no longer PRAY. For emptiness spawns violence, hatred, greed, malice, prejudice and every harbinger of non-being.
    The BODY of the Oblate, by her life of PRAYER is evidence of the LOVE, GRACE and INTEGRITY of GOD. GOD IS. I AM. PRAYER unites the human Spirit with the DIVINE NATURE. And yet I am not a Stranger to historical necessity. I witness both WITHIN and BEYOND time. The LIGHT of the GLORY guides interprets and transforms human existance. I am the embodiment of a prophetic priesthood. The thing the nations cannot anticipate, I speak it! And through my prayings I pursue the blessing of all NATIONS. The GLORY RESPONDS. THE GLORY Prevails.

ONE

"The secret things belong to the LORD our God, but the revealed things belong to us and to our children forever, to observe all the words of this law."

(Deuteronomy 29:29)

This LIVING within the "Glory of the Lord" has a peculiar bent of "practical" mysticism. For example, it's best not to talk back to angels out loud in public. Also One ought to avoid being candid about the scent of chaos when in the presence of "religious leaders." Third, it is helpful to those who banish or isolate you; if you "appear" not to notice the futility of their best efforts! And most important, it is better not to alarm your Spouse with everything you discern! Let GOD reveal it!

So much is apocalyptic—a mesh of symbols, spirits, history and personal experience—in one's encounter with the Supernatural. Yet everything we experience, we experience *IN the body*. The mind observes, interprets, communicates. But the SPIRIT transforms, eclipses and uncovers. The body is a witness!

LISTEN.

LISTEN to your BODY when it cries out to be released from anger, unforgiveness, fatigue, complacency. LISTEN to you Body's longing to express the music, the Love, the poetry, the prayer, the dance, the sorrow WITHIN. LISTEN to your body's search for memories of innocence, quiet, health, passion and unprotected dreams. LISTEN to your BODY as she experiences the Near-ness of GOD. Hears the VOICE of GOD. Receives the POWER of GOD. Waits . . . and Waits . . . and Waits for the *TOUCH* of GOD. LISTEN to your Body with your PRAYERS.

LISTEN.

ONE

"The GLORY of the LORD rises upon you." (Isaiah 60:1)

A casual glance at the reflection of our lives gathers up at once the flaws, the mistakes, the bad decisions, the thoughtless remarks and the incomplete attempts at creativity. "Unauthorized" biographers will surely note the evidence of instability, mood swings, phobias, introversion and a lust for fresh flowers. Nevertheless. The Glory Rises and these broken places are transformed into channels of light, revelation and healing for the nations. The GLORY Rises and an exhilirating RADIANCE shapes the pathos of my natural existence into a supernatural manifestation of the favor of the Lord. THE GLORY RISES and undisclosed power gifts of the Spirit enunciate themselves in a vocabulary of HOPE too GOD to be refuted. THE GLORY RISES and the perjured, violated body of an African-ancestored woman becomes the tabernacle of the MOST-HIGH GOD.

This is the GLORY; that *my* body which has been the locus of shame, the target of Evil. My cloister of sorrow. *My* body now stands at the center of the healing of the Universe. Eternity Past. Eternity Present. Eternity Future. The GLORY forever rises upon me. If you look only at what you see; you will depart with the chronicles of rejection—racial, sexual, theological, historical and personal. But, if you PRAY to Behold the GLORY, you will hear GOD speaking to your heart by faith. You too will begin to affirm in Joyous liberation:

THIS IS *MY* BODY.
May I never be ashamed!
THIS IS *MY* BODY.
MAY the GLORY of the LORD enfold ME
    FOREVER.
THIS IS *MY* BODY.
                    SELAH.

ONE — ANOTHER RHYTHM FOR LIVING

Sometimes our experiences in the Spirit realm defy "rational" categories. When this happens, we are reluctant to share them for fear of the "fanatics" crown. Yet, in praying through, I have found there is symmetry in the bowels of chaos. There is a message in "madness." There is a strange Beauty in the storm! And "reason" is not the highest standard of Divinity. If you are unprepared to take THIS PLUNGE right now, MOVE on to the next chapter.

Today I walked beside mySelf. Lunar strokes of madness taunted me; riddled my confidence with bullets of glass. Each one shattering upon impact. Splintering my Soul. Melancholia is not a lover easily abandoned. Tonight is the Night. Whispers of death echo in the forest of my thoughts. I no longer fear them. Tonight is the NIGHT. I will speak of my Realities. I can breathe Again!

> "Worthy is the Lamb
> that was slain . . .
> (Revelations 5:12)

There are no roadblocks here.
I wander an endless frontier.
No walls.
Unboundaried.
Sheer Sky. Platinum Moon.
The Purpose is in the moment.
> "Angels we have heard on high . . ."
In the snapshot of this moment.
My body is my friend.
No longer angry with me.
Rested.
Nourished.
Energized.
Tranquil.
I am no longer who I have been.
This is my body!

ONE

What must our LORD have been feeling when He uttered these sacred words; "This is my body." (Luke 22:19)? Was it passion?
Release?
Shame?
Fear?
Generosity?
HOPE?

    "THIS IS MY BODY." Can this be the lyrical
       incantation of suffering-LOVE.
    "THIS IS MY BODY." Perhaps the eternal
       articulation of a solidarity that won't quit!
    "THIS IS MY BODY." Is it the Self-offering of
       the Prayer of tangibility?
    "This is my Body."
    I want to learn to pray all over again!
    Pray in the bowels of the SPIRIT.
    To PRAY having been seized by the LOVE of God.
Ardently.
Enthusiastically.
In Silence.
In Tongues of Fire.
In tranquility.
With Reverence and
HOPE.

ONE

Praying to receive the Spirit of PRAYER has yielded a season of loss, mourning, oftimes an uncentered madness. But it has been the isolation to terror that most effectively paralysed my hope. My body, my friends, my relations, the church, the Vision—all enemies! And PRAYER did not come. And so you join me now in the paradox of this apostolate: that I am compelled to write concerning the thing I have not *fully* received!

I am gasping to speak to you. (For, Spiritually I am out of breath.) "My heart fainteth." (Genesis 45:26) There is an inimitable communion between body and soul. There is an incredible something that is ignited in the believer when the moment of awakening takes place. The physical is transposed. Yes, the blind see. The lame walk. The dumb speak. Wholeness rises from broken places, Eros births Agape. The natural collapses in the arms of the immortal. The Soul sings acappella. whoosh . . .

As the interior life is bathed in Splendor, Radiance signals humanity of the presence of the Elect. And there is no more FEAR.

Arms and feet, head and breasts, legs and lungs, fingers and toes embrace Heaven. The sky and the tongues of the ocean murmer ecstasies at the sight there of. I have found out my own secret. The body is the friend of prayer! Responding to the desires of the Spirit; signalling the promptings of the Spirit; housing the identity of the Spirit. "Know ye not that your body is the temple of the Holy Ghost . . .?" (1 Corinthians 6:19) I am the Space in which God lives. The living Space of God am I.

Every cell
    system
      faculty
        function
          organ
experience
    collaborate with; yield to; open unto; the praying moment. "Therefore be clear minded and self-controlled so that you can pray." (1 Peter 4:7) Emptied of every motive and conclusion; prayer is coming blindfolded to a surprise birthday party. When I enter, I have no knowledge of the guests who have arrived before me, but I sense their Christ presence, their longings concerning me. I am virtually "surrounded by a cloud of witnesses" (Hebrews 12:1) Unknown to me there are many unopened gifts that have been brought to the occasion just for me! Each has a purpose and communicates something concerning me and the Giver. Yet, I cannot speak, I must first be permitted to see. I do not flail my arms in the darkness, or lunge awkwardly into unknown spaces. I must be STILL. Although I am the honored guest, I must be "invited" to partake of the celebration.

    ". . . . offer your bodies as living sacrifices, holy and
    pleasing to God—this is your spiritual act of worship."
                                     (Romans 12:1)

Ah then, my body becomes a gift to prayer! This body is not spectator to the enthralling moment of conception. She is guest and host. Amen. "I don't know quite what to do with mySelf." How often have I lived this thought in uncomfortable, threatening and vulnerable moments? All having to do with the *perceived* rejection or condemnation of others. In prayer it is never so. I am *always* honored. Always heard. *Always* understood. *Always* respected. *Always* included. Amen. And my body responds willingly, passionately, freely as in the arms of a gentle, caring lover.

ONE

"Therefore prepare your minds for action; discipline yourselves; set all your hope on the grace that Jesus Christ will bring you when he is revealed."

(I Peter 1:13)

ONE

And so I want to pray. My soul, my heart, my mind, my will, my desires, my thoughts, my priorities, my fears prostate themselves before God, the living good. My body can do no other. Prostration is a Spiritual condition. In it the body suggests what the Soul confesses in Christ Jesus—

". . . Holy, holy, holy, the Lord God the Almighty, who was and is and is to come. And whenever the living creatures give glory and honor and thanks to the one who is seated on the throne, who lives forever and ever, the twenty-four elders fall before the one who is seated on the throne and worship the one who lives forever and ever; they cast their crowns before the throne, singing, You are worthy, . . ."

(Revelation 4:8b–11a)

This remarkable assent of the body to the move of the Spirit is a continuity of the paradigm in the heavenlies.

Reflect for a season on what it means to be "the LIVING SPACE of GOD."

**How will it impact your self-understanding,
relationships,
Prayer life,
Vision of the Future?**

ONE

Shall I continue to fear my body?
Shall I feign modesty when it is
disappointment that reigns?
Shall I risk looking at her with both eyes open?
    touching her with my heart?
    listening to her with my Soul?
    celebrating her with my imagination?
This is my body.
    She is more than fatigue, infirmity, cellulite, and the empty space where a womb used to be.
This is my body.
I am the bird of Paradise.
I am consort of the Lion of Judah.
I am a 12 winged accolade to African women who
    died while trying;
    cried beyond tears;
    loved when it hurt;
    and were falsely accused by their friends.
This body "lives, moves and has reality" (Acts 17:28) because of the Supreme Light. The LIGHT who shines within Himself. The LIGHT who has no Source. The LIGHT whose Self humiliation is to inhabit imperfection and render me Perfect. This LIGHT who stands within and against history, circumstance and reason Recreates meaning and Hope in the domicile of my great sorrow: death. Today I dance with God. Tomorrow will be its own testimony.
I want to speak of something I have no language for. I want to take custody of my own secrets—hidden/kept from myself.

ONE

So Let us ramble through the forgotten dreams of women who no longer know themselves. Who have fallen off the steep cliffs of rejection and now live in volcanic ashes. Who remain awake at midnight courting the storms of childhood memories. Whose lips turn to stone when it's time to Pray. Who cannot remember the names of their children or their lovers. Who don't know where their grandmothers are buried. Who retie their headrags over and over and over again because they can no longer love themselves. Who cannot feel the future. WHO welcome only Death. In the canyon of dreams there is music.
There are portraits.
There are precious gems.
There are unfinished curtains and novels; a thousand million poems.
There are altars, and awnings and nations to be governed.
There is the laughter of unborn babies.
And so many, many gardens.
There are unspoken apologies.
Journeys and classes and advice *not* taken.
Smiles and kindnesses that should have been given away.
Abandoned friendships,
    Causes,
and symphonies.
Neglected photographs,
    hanging plants,
and relations.
Pyramids of wonder.
Unnamed cures for plagues,
    fear, loneliness and
      the common cold!

ONE

Angels, confidantes and beautiful moments.
Cakes that should have been baked.
A bright yellow balloon that escaped my
young fingers.
A cup of tea with too much honey.
A dollar wasted with Joy.
A warm hug.
A sweet smile.
A gentle shower.
"This is My body broken for you . . .
except you eat of it, you cannot share
in the Kingdom of Heaven, saith the
Lord." (John 13:8)
"Take and eat."

BE SILENT.

He has given me His Body.
Now I offer Him mine.
    This is my body:
    A rhythm of Hope.
    an architecture of Destiny.
    the yoke of Providence.
    Your channel of Self revelation.
    Echo of Divine logos.
    shadow of Eternal Radiance.
    habitat of mortality.
    orchestral song of the generations.
    concubine of death.
    way station of infirmities.

ONE

"Keep my steps steady according to your promise, and never let iniquity have dominion over me."

(Psalm 119:133)

wellspring of creativity.
image of God.

There is something surrealistic about contemplating my own body.
Touching my own skin.
Inhaling my own scents.
Beholding The Woman!

The network of REJECTION that has distanced me from my own body is exposed. Today I will take off my shoes, my "success," my make up, my fear, my anger. Today I will stand Naked. I **AM** Holy Ground:

"before you were conceived in your mother's womb, I knew you . . ."
(Jeremiah 1:5)

ONE

Giving my Body to the Holy SPIRIT in Prayer
Encourages me.
Blesses me.
Illumines me.
Liberates me.
Heals me.
For my Body has vocabulary, memory, passion and expression. When I speak with my voice alone; I am silencing the greater part of mySelf. So much is locked away in the desperate, imposed silences of my Body life. I long to say with my BODY what my God-ward thoughts are. To experience my Body, sing, moan, laugh, petition and play with GOD. As a musician communes through her instrument so shall it be with my BODY.

> A continuous praying for deliverance from the spirit of self-rejection and criticism must accompany my steps along the way.

For within me are undisclosed universes of POWER to be released. I can feel the "magic" when I dance. I can taste the salty FIRE. Each cell is ignited. Every muscle infused. Every tissue soaked in Supernatural oils. My very bones are polished with Holy dew. My Soul perspires from the sanctifying adrenalin. This Body celebrates "Christ IN me, the Hope of Glory." (Colossians 1:27)

For those whose BODY PRAYERS remain unvoiced. I share with you mine. Allow them to encourage the Release of the prayers God desires. They are stored up in your Body. Lay before the Lord. Let the Spirit guide your hands to bless the parts of your body that call out to your soul.

A BODY PRAYER is a Prayer in which the Holy Spirit and the imagination give the body a vocabulary to speak with the LORD. The prayer is uttered in the language of the body. Not a word is spoken with the lips. This is TOTAL Prayer—mind, memory, idea, emotion, Spirit, every faculty, organ, sense, muscle, tissue, cell, passion, HOPE and mystery are released in the PRAYER ENCOUNTER.

MAY the PRAYER in You be Manifested. AMEN.

ONE   **BODY PRAYERS**

INVOCATION:

    Life of Christ
    Flow in me
    Flow in my Cardiovascular system
        ever more, ever more
    Flow in my Respiratory system
        ever more, ever more
    Flow in my Digestive system
        ever more, ever more
    Flow in my Neurological system
        ever more, ever more
    LIFE OF CHRIST
    Flow in me
        ever more, ever more.
    Make me ALIVE in
        you EVER MORE.
                              AMEN.

BEFORE SLEEPING:

"You who live in the shelter of the Most High, who abide in the shadow of the Almighty," (Psalm 91:1)

Holy One, LIFE OF JESUS;
    Ride my breath to inward places.
    Abide in me.
    Where sun, nor rain, nor freezing
        wind has ever touched.
    Abide in me.
    Unleash your energies
    in my imagination when I sleep.
    Abide in me.
    And awaken me to the Glorious Wonder
        of LIFE forever.
                              AMEN.

BODY PRAYERS

FOR INHABITATION:

God, this is my BODY.
She is an expression
of your Genius.
Give birth in my
Body to a
Spirit of
Exaltation, Wonder,
REVERENCE,
PRAISE and
      HOPE, In the Name of the
Father, the Son and the Holy Ghost.
                              Amen.

FOR PURIFICATION:

LORD, I want to LIVE in my Body.
Cleanse me of every
   fear: (name them)
   phobia: (name them)
   addiction: (name them)
   and
   disease.   (name them)
Help me to experience LIFE
in my heart,
fingers and toes,
bosom and legs
arms and head
buttocks and
lungs.
Let the Name of JESUS
ignite a quickening fire
in every cell in my body
                              Amen.

ONE

FOR DELIVERANCE: (A Continuous Prayer of the Heart):

LORD, Jesus,
I am bound
in my BODY,
Set me FREE.
Release me Holy SPIRIT.
Release me.
                Amen.

FOR RELEASE:

LORD, I don't want
to be
(ashamed) of [   ] (afraid) of [   ]
(angry) with [   ]
(estranged) from [   ]
my BODY
anymore.
Call me out of this
Tomb and I'll
come Dancing! with
ThanksGIVING. In the Name of Jesus.
                Amen.

FOR HEALING:

"Heal me O Lord and
I shall be Healed."
            (Jeremiah 17:14)
            Amen.

UPON RISING:

> Lord, I Give YOU my Body
> as a thank offering
> for your LOVE.
> Do with me that which
> pleases YOU.
> I consecrate every thought,
>   every gesture,
>   every movement,
>   to your Glory.

Whatever my eyes see; I bless with your name.
Whatever my hands touch, I shall bless in Your Name.
Whatever ground I stand on, I will occupy in your Name.
LET Eternity Pass THROUGH my loins this Day; and I shall redeem the NATIONS in JESUS' name.

                                     Amen.

WHILE MAKING LOVE (A Continuous Prayer of the HEART):

> LORD, we belong to YOU. Open us to each other's desire. Take the LONGING and the JOY to deeper realms than we have known before. Explode the boundaries of our imaginations. In each other's arms, let us go to Heaven **Before** we DIE. Pour down oils of Passion in our bodies and then ignite us with Eternal FIRE Ohhhh

ONE

ONE

"If the Spirit of him who raised Jesus from the dead dwells in you, he who raised Christ from the dead will give life to your mortal bodies also through his Spirit that dwells in you."
(Romans 8:11)

There is Life in my Body.
Holy.
Free.
Creative.
Beautiful.
Life.

The Resurrection is the unique Reality of the Christian Faith that bestows a HOPE that is both NOW and Eternal. The GLORY of the LORD abides in **this** mortal body, to be sure!

To pray is to RISE from the dead!
Know This. Prayer is experiential as well as transcendent. Prayer both wounds and heals. Prayer is the REALITY of GOD in the human predicament. From my Body, I Reach for GOD. In my Body, GOD
    finds me.
    touches me.
    speaks to me.
    blesses me.
Waits with me and for me.
May I never be ashamed (Again).
This is my Body.
The Living Space of God.

MOURNING INTO DANCING

I will "dig" deeper as I write.
Open UP more.
Change is necessary.
Change is process.
CHANGE HEALS.
I will write my way into Wholeness.

"MOURNING INTO DANCING" TWO

Reflect on the moment
when death came knocking—
Welcome or unwelcome
expected or UNEXPECTED.
Recapture the movements in
your Soul—
when Death came riding—
Riding through your world
Like an unbridled storm,
a treacherous Army.
Remember the awesome
Midnight become morning—
When death like the wind
blew into your dreams
and with its' icy fingers
froze your laughter,
     your song,
        and your memory of LOVE.
Now light a candle.
Blow it out.
Death is GONE.
LIFE IS HERE.
BE RENEWED.

          SELAH

TWO

"May those who sow in tears reap with shouts of joy."

(Psalm 126:5)

"They came to the other side of the sea, to the country of the Gerasenes."

(Mark 5:1)

The scent of FEAR has fled my nostrils. Serenity has replaced the pursuit of songs of happiness as my primary resolve. In fact, upon close inspection, I recognize that happiness was really not something I knew to desire for myself. This love affair with sorrow has been a long-standing relationship. Intense fidelity. No barriers. God was one of many *responsibilities*. A burden to be borne. An unfriendly suitor with an insurmountable list of demands. A RECLUSE. An indigo martyr. A mystery in Sapphire. A semi-previous jewel. A warden. A lost dream.

It was upon tasting the salted saliva of my own madness, that I left the quarry of Gerasene and renounced the perils of infirmity, fear, panic and desolation. I entered the open space. Breath for my soul. Music for my heart. Grace for my Body. The infrastructure of terror is being dismantled by the POWER of the Holy Spirit. Two days since my own personal PENTECOST, Tongues of FIRE rest on my Soul. Hope ignites a peculiar, quiet RELEASE. There are no "strangers" here. The whole of life is beauty. An aura of enchantment has seduced my melancholy temperment and bathes me in the Sacred Waters of LOVE.

Real Love and TRUE.

Undefiled.

There is no foreboding premonition.

Only Balance.

I am, after all, collaborating with GOD in the re-SHAPING of my life. Enthusiasm, Harmony, and Flow are the active ingredients.

    I am a WRITER. A writer must write.
    I am an ARTIST. An artist must have solitude.
    I am a Woman. A woman flowers in beautiful spaces.
    I am a PROPHET. A PROPHET must have time with GOD.
    I am AFRICAN. AFRICA is the genesis of HOPE.

Know Who YOU ARE!

TWO

The furor within subsides.
The didactic of HURT no longer reproduces itself as mistrust.
The wind blows through the hollow memory of the former things.
A mist of invocations rises from the dry and blistered lips of a Soul too parched to cry.
Death has passed from me.
My bowels are cleansed.
My heart is purged.
My thoughts are RADIANT.
GOD leaps in the HEAVENS.
GOD whirls through Hiroshima, Kigali, Danane, Estonia, and Yonkers.
Each the shadow of a nation in apocalyptic HOPE.
Each crying out for a Naked God.
My heart faces the East.
Messiah comes.
Surely Messiah Comes.
I leave the doors and windows open.
So that whether I am awake or asleep,
      living or dead,
         sterile or fecund,
           Messiah may enter.
How many Mondays make up a lifetime?
How many pairs of empty eyes?
How many discarded Ruthies?
How many polluted lakes?
How many defiled sanctuaries?
How many betrayals?

Know Who you ARE!
Seek GOD.
Enthusiasm, Harmony and Flow are the *active* ingredients of a Visionary Apostolate. We can never be as others are! We cannot walk in their footsteps; see through their windows or drink the wine of their expectations. Covetousness is the worst form of treachery. The greatest source of self sabotage.
Know WHO you ARE!
See GOD.

TWO

I am learning to be Passionate about
> the intangible,
> the obsequious,
> the plain,
> the stark,
> the simple,
> the hidden.

NATURE, IDEA, SCENT, COLOR. TEXTURE. LIGHT. WORD. SYMPHONY. PATTERN. A lion's hair. That which I cannot SEE is nonetheless Real. So it is with LOVE.
"LOVE keeps no Record of Wrongs." (I Cor. 13:5)
LOVE will not cohabitate with Death.
LOVE can let go.
Death holds on.
A Rainbow of tears sparkle like diamonds as the anointing delivers me from bondage.
Freedom is awesome!
I shall not "be entangled again with the yoke of bondage." (2 Peter 2:20)
In the Name of Jesus! What did it take to get here:
> incarnation
> flight into Egypt
> baptisms
> temptations
> the wilderness
> Gethsemane
> TRIAL
> Execution
> and Resurrection.

Sometimes one by one. Many times Simultaneously. The sequence is a matter of VISION and experience. Vision and Response. Life applauds itself when the courageous refuse to die. The duration of the "wake" exceeded the boundaries of necessity.
I rise by the power of God on the wings of effectual PRAYERS.
>	The prayers of JESUS,
>	The prayers of the intercessors.
>	The voluminous incense.
>	And my own inward assent to the Spirit of the LORD.

Further evidence that one does not PRAY "FOR" results. The Soul prays to touch GOD.
This GOD I feared.
>	Resented.
>	Mistrusted.
>	Fled.

This GOD whom I perceived as partial.
>	Unfriendly.
>	Blind.
>	Disinterested.

I waited for God.
>	Grieved over God.
>	"Defended" my limited knowledge of this GOD.

But these things have passed away!
And now I Dance with GOD.
I, a woman.
A woman in a Body.
My body.
I Dance with God.
The God who can now be touched. (John 20:17)
Whose Name can be spoken.
Voice can be heard.
Glory be revealed
Mysteries shared.
>	Tears felt and tasted.

TWO

"Surely now God has worn me out; he has made desolate all my company." (Job 16:7)

"For who is there of all flesh that has heard the voice of the living God speaking out of fire, as we have, and remained alive?"

(Deuteronomy 5:26)

TWO

"My spirit is broken, my days are cut short, the grave awaits me."

(Job 17:1)

To dance with GOD is a wondrous Healing thing. There is no synonym in my experience that evokes the PASSION, THE mystery, THE oceanic power of this moment. I am about to pass away into a MIDNIGHT of fire. I am sequestered in a Cosmic appeal for rhapsody. There is no sunlight equal to this Radiance. There is no prayer like death. No Sorrow like unto Love. No shadow like the grave. Death, Love and the Grave—these three—had destroyed my Hope; my very desire for God. My Soul wept night and morning for this reason. There were no choirs singing in memoriam. No candles lit to my memory. No litanies read over my heart. Rather a horde of vultures gathered to pick the meat from the bones of my very Soul. I breathed despair. Yet GOD would not let me die. Neither from betrayal, abuse, neglect, torment, fear, or infirmity. God refused me death's sweet pardon. And so I grieved with every ounce of strength that I had. I grieved through myriad paths of imagination. I grieved and mourned that I was yet alive in a condition that could only be recognized as death! Madness brings a deceptively gentle Peace until it's interrupted by God!

The LIGHT, the sound, the Power.
The midnight that changes me—changed EVERYTHING! I have been the sole attendee/mourner at my own wake for many years. And now I am admonished to depart. To pass out of the Chapel of the dying into the Tabernacle of the being born! Angels take me by the hand and "lead me gently on." Once death has become familiar, comfortable; LIFE is strange, awkward, difficult, embarrassing, lonely—mostly lonely. A sea of strangers stand at the gate: eyes daggers, lips smiling;
      withholding God from their prayers;
         whispering chaos;
   manipulating emotion;
      destroying heaven with empty hymns.

I will surge through them. Beyond the grasp of their deception. There are streams of Holiness flowing from the River of God. I will bathe in these waters and be made whole. I will remember the former things not again!

> "Search me, O God,
> and know my heart;
> test me and know my thoughts.
> See if there is any wicked way in me,
> and lead me in the way everlasting."
>
> (Psalm 139: 23, 24)

God has decided that *my* time has come!
God is smoothing the wrinkles in my expectation.
God is being conspicuous about my deliverance.
If only I knew how to pray. If only my prayer life becomes my LIFE. Let me pray prayers of ascent and I will touch the throne of GOD. Too many believers trapped in the delusion of religion. Martyred by ambition, they exchange the anointing for "name recognition"—their own! I must ascend. Flow inward, upward, beyond, when I am in PRAYER.

"SPEAK TO MY HEART, HOLY SPIRIT."

I must ascend. I shall ascend. Beyond this death delusion is my hemisphere of Blessing. I feared "success" in the hands of the LORD. For one too impoverished for nobility. TOO intelligent for innocence. TOO passionate to be objective. Too UNFORGIVING to be gracious. Certainly, I could not be the One! Years of self-imposed penance never assuaged my anxieties. But rather caused them to multiply.

I must ASCEND. I shall ascend. This is NOT a "dress rehearsal." This is my LIFE!

Dear Cojourner, Let us seek NOW the LORD. Let us inquire of GOD's wisdom.

TWO

TWO

"Neither is new wine put into old wineskins; otherwise, the skins burst, and the wine is spilled, and the skins are destroyed; but new wine is put into fresh wineskins, and so both are preserved."

(Matthew 9:17)

What is the nature, meaning and experience of PRAYERS of ASCENT? This is what I received as an answer:

PRAYERS of ASCENT disengage my SOUL LIFE from the vernacular of mortality. These prayers must cause me to surge like propelling waters to the high ground of FAITH. These prayers must listen to the SILENCE; see in the darkness; water arid gardens of hope. These prayers must incarnate, crucify and resurrect the VISION. These prayers render mute the orator, the homiletician, the diplomat, the barrister. These prayers delve into realms of the fore-knowledge of GOD and burst old wineskins! These PRAYERS demystify the Canon. Rank with the oracles of GOD. "Lay aside every weight and the sin that doth so easily beset us . . ." (Hebrew 12:1) THESE PRAYERS make my SOUL RUN—

"Run and not get weary!" (Isaiah 40:31)
"RUN with horses!" (Jeremiah 12:5)
"RUN for the PRIZE." (1 Cor. 9:24)
"RUN with PATIENCE . . . (Hebrews 12:1)

It is an interior flight of supernatural proportions! But one that I must take, if I am to break free of this "unconsecrated" death. Only those who KNOW can understand. This is a death *within* mortality. NOT beyond it!

> "I shall not die,
> but I shall live,
> and recount the deeds of the LORD."
> *(Psalms 118:17)*

LET US PRAY TO LIVE.
LET us PRAY to be quickened—
    in the deep places of our imagination,
    beneath our scab covered wounds,
    down the staircase of our memory.
LET US PRAY with hearts outstretched
    and baptismal tears
    til the quaking of our souls.
LET US PRAY TO LIVE.
    TO LOVE.
    TO Dream.
    FOREVER.
        Amen.

This is not a matter of Resurrection. This is a matter of SOULhealth,
The knowledge that I CAN be healed, am being
Healed—
quickens me!
motivates me!
delights me!
protects me!
LIBERATES me!

    For those who mourn, there comes a TIME to HEAL. There is something at once compelling and fearsome about this realization. NEW LIFE AWAITS ME.
STRENGTH.
BEAUTY.
GRACE.
AGILITY.
WONDER.
NEWNESS!
What will it be like?
Am I READY?
Will I be Able to sustain it?
Will it be MINE?

> **The response of the Holy SPIRIT is to lead me to the HEALING CIRCLE through invocations of the heart:**
> **"Come LORD Jesus, Come." (Revelation 22:20)**
> **"HEALING FIRE of GOD ARISE in me."**
> **"HEALING Mercy of GOD infuse me with your**
>   **PRESENCE."**
> **"HEALING LOVE of JESUS, I surrender mySelf to YOU:**
>   **MIND, BODY AND SOUL."**
>   **The oblate must ever invoke the Healing Circle. For it is *within* the Healing Circle that the Holy SPIRIT teaches me the mysteries of my own HEALING.**

TWO

"Beloved, I pray that all may go well with you and that you may be in good health, just as it is well with your soul."

(3 John 1:2)

THE HEALING CIRCLE

1. As you pass into the Healing Circle, be fully present to the activity of GOD.

TWO

"O LORD our God, other lords besides you have ruled over us, but we acknowledge your name alone."

(Isaiah 26:13)

"If the Spirit of him who raised Jesus from the dead dwells in you, he who raised Christ from the dead will give life to your mortal bodies also through his Spirit that dwells in you."

(Romans 8:11)

I speak the NAME of JESUS,
Close my eyes,
Center my SPIRIT at the foot of His cross.

By the Name of "JESUS" I repel every distraction.
Through His Name, "JESUS," I enter the HEALING CIRCLE.
(No matter where I am.
No matter what is going on around me.)
I ENTER THE HEALING CIRCLE:

"In the NAME of JESUS CHRIST,
SON of GOD,
Messiah.
WHOSE Blood has redeemed
Repentant Humanity.
I am "filled with the fullness of GOD." (Ephesians 3:19)
I surround myself NOW
with the FAVOR of the LORD,
I surround myself with the vitality
of the WORD of GOD.
I surround mySelf with Faith in
my capacity to respond to the
Healing available to me "NOW."
AMEN.

As I pray, I begin to see a hoop of flames in a sea of blackness. I am at PEACE.

I continue to pray:

> In the NAME of Jesus Christ
> the Son of God,
> Redeemer.
> Whose Name is above every other NAME in earth
> under the earth
> and in the heavens.
> I surround myself with FORGIVENESS
> The forgiveness That JESUS, Himself
> prayed for me to receive.
> The forgiveness, I allow God
> to express through me to those
> who have harmed me and
> those whom I have harmed.
> THE FORGIVENESS I offer
> mySELF
> for betraying my PURPOSE.

The flames of the HOOP surge inward.
I cannot see myself.
But I hear names.
The same names again and again.
The sting is gone!
Healing FIRE swallows me.

TWO

2. *GIVE yourself to the Holy Spirit, when you Pray.*

"So Pilate gave his verdict that their demand should be granted."

(Luke 23:24)

TWO

3. *Experience the Union and vocation of the TRINITY.*

I can't stop PRAYING:
> **In the Name of JESUS CHRIST,**
> **SON of GOD,**
> **Messiah.**
> **WHOSE NATURE**
> **and MOTIVE**
> **and VOCATION is LOVE.**
> **I surround myself with**
> **the LOVE of God.**
> **I empty mySelf and my space**
> **of every conflicting emotion,**
> **passion,**
> **urge,**
> **I am Filled by the LOVE of GOD.**
> **I LOVE the LORD with All**
> **my heart,**
> **mind,**
> **Soul and**
> **strength.**
> **I Love others.**
> **I Love mySelf.**
> **By this LOVE, I receive LOVE:**
> **the LOVE of TRINITY**
> **the LOVE OF others**
> **Self Love.**
> **Immortal in Creation!**

A greater, more brilliant fire descends upon the hoop of flames.

The darkness is silenced.
    LOST.
   swallowed up in LOVE's fires.

THE Healing Circle is Perfect.
    Eternal.
  can only be broken, interrupted or extinguished by
MY failure to believe or
MY rebellion against forgiveness or
MY denial of LOVE.

Healing PRAYER is the breath of Heaven on
the restless and wounded Soul.
To be Healed is to enter completion,
    the realm of belonging
The name of **JESUS** is the passageway to
    the Healing Circle.

I step into the Center of the Healing Circle
by the SPIRIT of the LORD singing:
    I believe in GOD
    the Almighty Creator.
    Of one Reality
    with Jesus CHRIST
    and the
    HOLY GHOST.

    I believe I am NOW

TWO

4. *Affirm in your Heart.*
   I BELIEVE.
   I FORGIVE,
   I Obey.

TWO

5. LIVE in this PRAYER. And then Honor the SILENCE until you are RELEASED.

and Eternally
fully present to
the REGENERATING
LOVE of
GOD
that issues from
the very utterance of
the name of
JESUS.

I believe that by FAITH
in
Jesus CHRIST,
the Power of FORGIVENESS
and the effectual
work of DIVINE LOVE;

I Receive supernaturally—
HEALING
of SPIRIT
MIND,
BODY,
and EMOTION.

Now it is time for SILENCE.
Stillness.
SPIRIT work.

6. CLOSE with THE LORD'S PRAYER.

7. ARISE, you are being "made whole!"

TWO

The Healing Circle by virtue of its RADICAL inclusiveness teaches Holiness in the most profound sense.
This is Holiness.
To LOVE those who harm you,*
   more than you love your own body.
To LOVE GOD incessantly.
To LOVE mySelf as chosen, elect, a GIFT of GOD.
To LOVE creation.
To LOVE humanity with all our flaws and graces.
   With all our depravity and kindness.
Only then is the warfare ended and the life of the body ignited.
    For THE DANCE is born in LOVE.
       Sustained in LOVE.
       and by LOVE manifested.
    To DANCE with GOD,
I must be abandoned to LOVE.
There is no Death in LOVE.
Mourning days and nights are ended.
I am Healed.
LOVE has made ME whole.

THE HEALING VOCATION

SPIRIT alone Heals. Not personality, Ritual or doctrine. SPIRIT Heals. The Oblate prays to be a *channel through* which the Healing Love of GOD elects to flow to others. The ARTIST prays to be a *vessel through* which the SPIRIT elects to Express DIVINITY and so shall the world be healed. The Priest prays to *receive* an anointing *to Speak* the WORD of the SPIRIT that gifts healing to GOD's people. SPIRIT alone Heals.

"LOVE" also means taking back the power to "allow" our beloved to continue to do us harm.

TWO

"For an angel went down at a certain season into the pool, and troubled the water: whosoever then first after the troubling of the water stepped in was made whole of whatsoever disease he had."

(John 5:4 KJV)

In the silence, the SPIRIT speaks to me and my Heart prays in FAITH—

> **"HEAL me O Lord
> and I SHALL
> be Healed.
> Save me and I
> SHALL
> be SAVED.
> For Thou art
> my PRAISE."** (Jeremiah 17:14)

I cannot say how it happens, or even when. But HEALING comes! For some it may be dramatic. Apocalyptic even. Mine has been a JOB-esque encounter with time and Eternity. Humanity and DIVINITY. The Supernatural and the HISTORICAL. Word, World and Wonder are extant within my Soul. Pray and follow the urging of the Holy Spirit through four movements that will create an interior transformation.

(1) Humiliation: wounded unto strength

(2) Isolation: solitude as GIFT

(3) Abdication: In the Sovereignty of GOD there is no equal

(4) Revelation: LIVE to Behold the GLORY of the LORD.

HUMILIATION

PRAY:
"Wounds of Christ Sanctify me."

Amen

This is a remarkable praying encounter that awakens every "natural" compulsion to *rebellion*. Quite honestly the foundations of my self-esteem "quake" under the impact of this "call." The need for encouragement, companionship, autonomy and "facts" sustain the humanity of those with a leadership anointing! Without these, one trespasses from the mere realm of vulnerability into regions of powerlessness. When the virtue of HUMILITY is robed in the garment of Humiliation, my heart is torn open. Every raw impulse is exposed.

Is there life
        decency
        "Self"-respect
    beyond this moment?

There is an ascent in Prayer whereby the wound itself calls out to GOD. And GOD answers.

Secondly, basic to the human experience is the thrust toward inclusion. The veracity of union. Community is the authentic parable of the Kingdom of God on earth.
When we are denied
        excluded
        rejected
        Isolated;
the Soul itself is tormented. Unless by prayers of ascent we who are alone encounter GOD, who is also Alone. Divine solitude is the encounter between the Oblate who possesses nothing and the LORD of all emptiness. God receives my tears. I receive God's fullness.

The experience of one's own emptiness is nothing short of terrifying! ABDICATION means I surrender my "rights" even to the full knowledge of my MORTALITY. Here, the Oblate MUST pray for a spirit of obediance to the LORD. Pray to be governed by the UNCONTESTED authority of the WORD of GOD. Pray to ascend to a level of TRUST that is framed in UNCONDITIONAL LOVE!

The reluctance of many Cojourners is because of an inability "to SEE" GOD!
    The LOVE of GOD.
    The POWER of GOD.
    The TRUTH of GOD.
They have not experienced the Universe open itself to the FAITH of the Oblate. Neither have they "heard" the flapping of the wings of "Ministering Angels." Reason is their threshold. Doctrine their window. And Passion is constrained. What can carry such a Soul beyond this?
Only Prayer.
Prevailing PRAYER.
Intentional PRAYER.
      PRAYER THAT OPENS the Soul.
                     the Heart.
                     the LIFE.
                     the MIND.
                     the EYES.
SILENCE. HOLY SILENCE. CONSECRATED SILENCE. This is the echo of every prayer of ascent. This SILENCE is the altar of GOD in the Soul advancing in PRAYER.

TWO

ISOLATION

PRAY:
"Wounded CHRIST Embrace Me."

                Amen

ABDICATION

PRAY:
"I bow to the LORD, wounded for me."

                Amen

REVELATION

PRAY:
"WOUNDS of CHRIST SPEAK TO ME."

                Amen

TWO

The negativity and uncertainty associated with HUMILIATION, ISOLATION, ABDICATION and REVELATION are dissipated by the POWER of the Holy Spirit. We gain the capacity to see and Respond to Life in new and previously undiscovered ways. We are raised above culture, circumstance and personality. We will have grown higher on the inside. It is a matter of ascent. The hindering spirits of pride, insecurity, anxiety, loneliness and ambition are exposed and rebuked!

LET US PRAY TO THE LORD:

"LORD, take me Higher in THEE.
LORD, take me Higher in FAITH.
LORD, take me Higher in GRACE."

AMEN.

THE POWER AND MEANING OF ASCENT

TWO

PRAYER is an inward-upward Apostolate. Consider this: The "eye level" of the Soul in relation to GOD, is as a Palm Tree compared to Kilamanjaro. In PRAYER, I am constrained to see "beyond." To experience "beyond." To know "beyond." Thus I consciously surge past every limiting reality—whether political, emotional or natural. GOD is not "grounded" by the finitude of human culture. "GOD is SPIRIT."

(John 4:24)

The SPIRIT of GOD is as winged-Breath. Always calling us; compelling us; carrying us; provoking us; to unanticipated horizons. GOD breathes life into the Universe, the Church and the Oblate. This breath may come in the form of Word, Light, experience, miracle or even a supernatural awakening. Once *aware* of the *movement* of GOD's Spirit, how wonderful to *center*—allow oneself to be surrounded by the *Breath* and yield to its power. To inwardly *RELEASE* and *FLOW* in the energy of Divine LOVE. The Soul is always guided upward. Upward in faith. Upward in Humility. UPWARD in our capacity to endure suffering. The result is a *HIGHER* Knowledge of GOD. The Soul's deepest desire.

LET US ASCEND . . .

Prepare to meditate Aware, *Aloud* in 4 movements of ascent. There is great benefit in taking several deep breaths prior to the meditation. Observe a season of SILENCE at the conclusion of each meditation. (Remember, this is *not* a text book. This is a CoJourney in Prayer.) When you give yourself to the SILENCE of GOD; space is provided to write what you hear/see/experience. You may want to date your reality for future reference.

TWO

"I center myself in the flow of the breath of God."

1) **HUMILIATION**
"He has made me a byword of the peoples, and I am one before whom people spit. My eye has grown dim from grief, and all my members are like a shadow." (Job 17:6,7)

I embrace and release the unmerited condemnation.
I confess in my heart that "GOD is in Control."
I withdraw every emotional deposit I have made in this situation.
I render it powerless over me.
I place it in the heart of GOD for God to heal.
I bathe myself in the LOVE of God.
I silence "the accuser" with the Name of JESUS.
I give my heart to SILENCE.
I REST in the LORD.

"I give myself to the silence of GOD."

"I center myself in the flow of the breath of God."   TWO

2) **ISOLATION**
"when I was in my prime, . . . the friendship of God was upon my tent;" (Job 29:4)

I embrace and honor this Solitude.
I listen to the lessons it teaches me.
I am thankful for the new dimensions of mySelf
    that are being nurtured.
I renounce vengeance—it is the LORD's.
I renounce envy—it is impure.
I renounce guilt—it is unholy.
I invoke Serenity.
I invoke Harmony.
I invoke REST.
I am Healed.

"I give myself to the silence of GOD."

TWO

"I center myself in the flow of the breath of God."

3. **ABDICATION**
"Then Job answered the LORD: See, I am of small account; what shall I answer you? I lay my hand on my mouth. I have spoken once, and I will not answer; twice, but will proceed no further."
(Job 40:3–5)

I embrace and surrender to the Wisdom of GOD.
This moment is in the Path of Eternity.
I open mySelf to the GRACE of GOD.
I welcome the CHRIST-meaning of my LIFE.
I throw off pride.
I throw off ambition.
The priorities of the Kingdom are my TREASURE.
I open my hands,
    my heart,
    my mind,
    my LIFE to receive the WILL OF GOD
today and Forever.

"I give myself to the silence of GOD."

"I center myself in the flow of the breath of God."   TWO

4. **REVELATION**
   "I had heard of you by the hearing of the ear, but now my eye sees you;" (Job 42:5)

I embrace the REALITY of my Healing.
I shall see the LORD.
I shall perceive the hand of GOD.
I shall discern the PRESENCE of the Eternal.
I shall BEHOLD the RADIANCE of His GLORY.
I shall SEE the LORD.

"I give myself to the silence of GOD."

TWO

> "... mourning and crying and pain
>   will be no more,
> for the first things have passed
>   away."
>
> (Revelation 21:4)

Surely the paramount issue of faith is the matter of SUFFERING. How to face it without surrendering to it. How to resist the eager temptation to *spiritualize* it. Yet, refuse to dialogue with it *on its own terms.* The POWER of Ascent is not conferred upon the monastic only. But rather those who witness in the world with Holy LOVE and Prophetic Courage are able to confess as well a transcending urgency that shapes their lives.

"For this slight momentary affliction is preparing us for an eternal weight of glory beyond all measure."

(2 Corinthians 4:17)

Having experienced the whisper of the sovereignty of GOD;
  the Soul is healed.
  the life is healed.
  the body is healed.
  the mind is healed.
  the Church is healed.
  the Nations are healed.

"and be kind to one another, tenderhearted, forgiving one another, as God in Christ has forgiven you."

(Ephesians 4:32)

This healing movement is known as the DANCE of Reconciliation. The grieving and heaviness of heart that constricted our expression in acts of love dissolve into a reflection pool around which we can meditate on the GRACE of God. The power of this Dance is that each time we reach for a new partner! Each time we discover greater heights of freedom. Who will you welcome into the Healing Circle?

Name them and let the Dance begin!

-
-
-
-
-

(The person need not be *physically* present or even living for that matter!)

TWO

BELOVED COJOURNER;

Let us not give our sorrow the POWER to keep us from DANCING. Pain is fertile ground in which new rhythms and images can be planted. Watered with PATIENCE and HOPE, new relationships will spring forth. New Experiences will blossom.

In our mourning, we can learn the Healing POWER of DANCE. Great Blessing comes to the one who is not too ashamed to Dance alone.

Say to your sorrow:
"Nevertheless, I will Dance!"
Say to your disappointment:
"Nevertheless, I will Dance!"
Say to your regret:
"Nevertheless, I will Dance!"

When you Dance, GOD will DANCE with you.
For to Dance is an act of FAITH that cannot be denied!
FAITH in the INTEGRITY of Life.
FAITH in your own human potential.
FAITH in the mercies of GOD.
FAITH that your prayers have been heard.

"looking to Jesus the pioneer and perfecter of our faith, who for the sake of the joy that was set before him endured the cross, disregarding its shame, and has taken his seat at the right hand of the throne of God."

(Hebrews 12:2)

DEAR GOD,

SANKOFA BALLET

LORD HEAL THESE MEMORIES:

**WRITE
A PRAYER FOR THOSE WHO HAVE NO MEMORY
OF BEING LOVED:**

THREE

SANKOFA BALLET

"Long ago God spoke to our ancestors in many and various ways by the prophets," (Hebrews 1:1)

What songs are sung of the PAST!
What great feats proclaimed.
What mysteries and secrets are consigned to it.
What tremendous influence it lobbies for the future.
The PAST is romanticized. avoided. pursued.
      discarded. rationalized. celebrated.
      maligned. heralded. mourned. forgotten.
      misrepresented. imitated. refuted.
The PAST IS "fuzzy."
      hidden.
      silent.
      dominating.
      pleasant.
      cruel.
Most of all, it is **with** us!
      Shall we dance with the PAST? PRAY in the Past tense?
      We shall. We can. We must; If we are to be Healed.
      GOD is *in* our PAST: speaking, waiting,
            moving, waiting, listening, waiting . . .
      GOD is in our PAST: revealing, unveiling,
            awakening, manifesting . . .
      GOD is in our PAST: creating, redeeming,
            transforming. Healing. Healing. Healing.
SANKOFA teaches us the DANCE of Forward RETURN. "where the Spirit of the LORD is, there is freedom." (2 Corinthians 3:17)
Without fear, let us desire to lay hold of this "GIFT."
Let us offer ourselves to our un-named PAST.

THREE

Why should I return to that which I cannot change?
How can I find meaning/integrity/hope at the seat of what I perceive
    as my undoing?
Is there an unclaimed Vision in the past for a people
    who have been scourged by the nations?
Can the past shore up our HOPE/NEED/DESIRE for
    God to "arouse Himself" and shake the oppressor?
Will the Kingdom Come?
        REALLY?!

For many Cojourners our response to the Past is multifaceted. In some instances, the past is a dark room painted with remorse. Yet, there are moments when the past is a hurricane on the shores of a star-covered beach. Tragedy and Beauty joined together. The past can rush in on us with just the taste of a Milky Way Candy Bar. Or when fumbling with the dial on the radio you catch the last few notes of Marvin Gaye's "What's Goin On?" The past can envelop us with a mere whif of a certain tobacco in a room or the sight of little black patent leather shoes on Easter Sunday Morning.

    In your Past, there may be TERROR
                    CREATIVITY
                    SILK
                    INCEST
                    ANEMONES
                    FRIENDSHIP and/or
                    DANCE.
                    RAINBOWS.
                    WELFARE.
                    WARFARE.
                    MUSIC.
                    SILENCE.

THREE

But the most incredible moment in life for me was when I discovered **GOD** in my PAST. My Soul is inebriated with HOPE, whenever this realization captures my heart.

    Search your past for GOD.
    Look in broken places
    Torn down sheds.
    A passing smile.
    That strong hand on your shoulder.
    A door held open.
    A loaf of day-old bread "sold" for FREE!
    Someone who sits beside you even when
        Everyone else doesn't want to.
    A Rainy Day.
    A Sunny Day.
    A Plane held still during AIR turbulence
        because you're too tired to have to
        be AFRAID!
    God is amazingly alive and compassionate in your PAST.

Return and Seek GOD.
    Accept GOD.
    Worship GOD.
    Wonder with GOD.
    Surrender to GOD.

And the Universe will respond. The Universe will welcome you into it's bosom—the TRUE CHURCH.

Begin to PRAY.
PRAY into your past.
Begin to PRAY.
PRAY from the Heart of GOD.
Sense GOD's mood and GOD's move.
Embrace your destiny.

Oh to PRAY. To Dance. To be one with the LORD.
Oh just to be centered in the awareness of Divine purpose!
Oh to reach morning without travelling through the cynic's dread.

Holy Release certainly comes in the Sankofa Ballet—the forward movement that is birthed in homage to the Past. There is a way to the Past that leads through fire; another through barren desolation; and there may be many deep rivers on the journey. But every so often, there is a clear garden path, a candle lit road or an angelic guide. The latter are the sweet treasure of PRAYER.

Looking at photographs of myself from years ago, I can see the thick mask of depression; eyes filled with terror; a body rigid with anger, I SEE the war of my own Soul upon my face.

I walk to the mirror NOW, and I see GOD smiling back at me.
WE WON! Halleluia. We Won.

**Dear Cojourner,
If you are not ready to
lift the veil that
covers your Past, move
on to Chapter four.**

**May the PEACE of GOD
be with you to Comfort
you and to Bless you.**
                       AMEN

THREE

"The light of the body is the eye: if therefore thine eye be single, thy whole body shall be full of light."

(Matthew 6:22)

THREE

To my Cojourner:

LET us now pray to the LORD to be Open
to our PAST in all its dimensions.

Let us Pray the Holy Spirit to guide
us and illumine us and Heal us.

Let us Pray the Power of the Scriptures
to strengthen and establish us.

Let us Pray in the Words of David:

> "I fear no evil;
> for you are with me;
> your rod and your staff—
> they comfort me."
>
> (Psalms 23:4b)

Sit Quietly and allow the reality and meaning of these prayings to lay hold of your thought realm and Superintend your emotions.
    When this has happened;
        pray the LORD's PRAYER and BEGIN.

A thought at a time.
A page at a time.
A day at a time.
Let the Holy Spirit be your guide.

THREE

The Dance of RETURN is one of mounting intensity and must be performed with both skill and devotion. Prayers concerning the past are either framed in Doxologies or DIRGES. In either case, the Seeker can gain momentum of Soul simply by holding on to the VISION of Christ crucified. My personal particular past, my collective past and my Eternity past, have a way of unfurling in the wind of PRAYER.

And so I PRAY. I pray to ascend to the depths of Divinity. I PRAY. I pray to hear an end to mortal songs of despair. I PRAY. I pray to perceive the supernatural in my histories. I PRAY. I pray for language, humility and a fierce determination to LOVE again! A conversion of feelings ushers forward a Passionate Discipleship. The Divinity of Jesus both summons me and waits with me while I decide. With the very first step, I am made "new."

The "newness" is JESUS as Reality.
- as Soul mate
- as CoJourner in the MYSTERY
- as WINDOW to Eternity
- as Unconditional Presence

Yes, I am finally getting to know JESUS. Beyond, the all too familiar hymns. The memorized liturgies. I find mySelf "courting" His Spirit. Attempting to woo Him with naked repentances and the perfumed oils of Praise. I cry out to Him with accolades of blessing. I prostrate my Soul and my Body.

The implications of having a "personal" saviour awaken hidden meanings in my soul life. Spiritually, my prayer life had been "cued" to the drama and priorities of the congregation. I am somehow distanced from that in so many ways now. And at the same time, I am blessed with a deeper more authentic compassion.

I desire JESUS. My soul follows with deep longing His every gesture. Clings to His thoughts. Grieves for His Touch. Lies awake for His voice.

"So if anyone is in Christ, there is a new creation: everything old has passed away; see, everything has become new!"

(2 Corinthians 5:17)

THREE

"Listen, you that are deaf; and you that are blind, look up and see!"

(Isaiah 42:18)

"For forty years I loathed that generation and said, "They are a people whose hearts go astray, and they do not regard my ways."

(Psalms 95:10)

Because more than wealth or fame, I want to be the "Praise of His Glory." The woman God can talk to when God gets lonely or frustrated. The woman who wipes God's tears, shares God's JOYs and who is not too embarrassed to be God's public companion. In getting to know JESUS, more and more, I am beginning to joyfully accept mySelf! To sort out who I am from the misfit the culture had created. She was walking around in my body. Wearing my shoes! But *not* taking in any of the LIGHT I was receiving. In a lot of ways, she could have been mistaken for me, even by ME! I know now that she is not. Redemption had NO impact on her. Lonely shadow of a woman. Never knowing day from night. LOVE from manipulation. Life for her was a series of crises strung together by beads of betrayal. She cannot die because she never lived. I have slipped from her embrace. I have glimpsed the moon dancing. Seen the star rising in the East! I know where I am. I understand NOW why I am here. There can be no fatalities among the "awakened." We will live forever! As "stones of remembrance"

(Joshua 4:7)

    a "living HOPE"
    an untimely VISION
    a "grain of wheat"
    "bread cast upon the waters"
    "an empty tomb"
The Reality is JESUS.
        CHRIST.
        Son of God.
        Immortal.
        Messiah.
        Womb of GOD.
        LIGHT.
        Lion of Judah.
        FIRE of Prophecy.

Eternal
Everlasting.
FOREVER.
ENDLESS.
NOW.

The past has only beginnings for me NOW. I relinquish all sense of limitation. I extricate my future from the negotiating table of institutions, committees and personal pride. I resuscitate my childhood dreams. Liberate the Church from obscurity. Shatter the wall of SILENCE erected by my "friends" and enter the flame of illumination. This must be "Future Shock!"

I have set mySelf free from the press of conflicting goals, overlapping deadlines, psychological manipulation. I have met JESUS. And PRAYER is my heart's true vocation. So I banish mySelf from the courts of the Status Quo. I won't go back! I will not yield ground. I refuse to cave in to the pressures of assimiliation. I am on Eternity TIME.
Who can hurry me NOW?
WHO can Rush me awkwardly in a direction
    I do not care to travel?
WHO Can Crush my Soul?
    I know who JESUS Really is.
Jesus Christ IS the Son of God.
I know HE is.
As His Holiness penetrates the borders of my isolation, all I can see is Peace and Compassion. All I can hear is His voice. And He calls Me! Yes, He does. JESUS calls me by my new name.

THREE

"Now when all the people were baptized, and when Jesus also had been baptized and was praying, the heaven was opened, and the Holy Spirit descended upon him in bodily form like a dove. And a voice came from heaven, "You are my Son, the Beloved; with you I am well pleased."

(Luke 3:21,22)

THREE

"The Father loves the Son and shows him all that he himself is doing; and he will show him greater works than these, so that you will be astonished."

(John 5:20)

Saying, "Come unto Me." (Matthew 11:28)
    "Come unto Me."
    "Come unto Me."
The Past is swallowed up in the Eternity of Now.
My Soul is encouraged.
My Joy is awakened.
There is Real Transformation in the PRESENCE of Jesus.
The ARTIST becomes the Portrait.
The POET becomes the Poem.
The SINGER becomes the Song.
The Dancer becomes the Dance.
With what am I to compare this MIRACLE?
I am a Woman.
I am a LIVING Soul. I am Healed. This is LOVE. Boundless LOVE. Evoking prayers of fidelity and commitment. To know LOVE has been my soul desire. To taste it's delicacies. To be immersed in its waters. To stand naked in its LIGHT. There is no material trinket, high profile success, or conferred influence that I would accept in exchange for this LOVE. This LOVE has Supernatural Reality.
I shall in PRAYER return to LOVE'S beginnings.
I am flung into the Palace of TRINITY. The Palace of TRINITY is the abode in Prayer where Father, Son, and Holy Ghost are fully Visioned. There is Supernatural Completion and my Soul is at REST.
    Three voices; but ONE Word.
    Three realities; but ONE Space.
    Three movements, but ONE Power.
    This Place is a luminous, Timeless, BREATH. The PURPOSE of God, the WORD of GOD and the SPIRIT of GOD are ONE. I must bow down before the LORD. I cannot comprehend this moment. It is Perfect LOVE. [1 John 4:16]
There is no other explanation for the Mystery, the persona, the magnitude, POWER, the integrity or the DELIGHT of Love. Jesus will teach me.
"Come and See", He says. And my heart follows. I pursue the LORD. Going inward to go Higher. Drawing in of His Spirit to be sustained for the journey. God is NOT Dead. The imprint of God's fingerprints and footsteps are still warm upon creation.

My heart pursues the LORD in prayer. Sitting as a cross-legged insomniac before dawn waiting for God to appear. Pacing the corridors of my failures looking for a Sign. Startled by the shadows of my guilt crying for deliverance. Trying to part the "Red Sea" so African peoples can cross over into Destiny. I must follow close upon the heels of JESUS. Because His LOVE revives me when I grow faint. I pursue the Lord. I want to see the LIGHT. Touch the wound in His side. Hear His Voice.

"Come," He says. It is direct. Personal. Sincere. I am coming. This is my SOUL desire NOW. I am Coming! My body has been energized by the invitation. (Unexpected, but hoped for.) I will not tire of following after God. My dignity has been aroused. I will unlearn myself of all the cycles of mediocrity, visionlessness, and conformity. I have returned. I will step into Destiny. I have looked back. I will leap into tomorrow's song; I have remembered. I will follow the Son. This Dance is not strange to me. The unrehearsed finale is part of the repertoire of the Kingdom. My body recalls the graceful PROSTRATIONS. The applause of the "Cloud of witnesses" is a soft din within my Soul. I know why God comes to this dance with an entourage! I shall storm into the present age with a formidable determination to enjoy Holiness. No more dirges. No more blues. Sing me a LOVE song. "Let the daughters of Judah be glad." (Psalms 48:11)

Shout.

Jump for JOY.

"Softly, and tenderly Jesus is Calling"
(A.M.E. Hymnal, Hymn 261)

THREE

"Our God comes and does not keep silence, before him is a devouring fire, and a mighty tempest all around him."

(Psalms 50:3)

THREE

"Take care that you do not despise one of these little ones; for, I tell you, in heaven their angels continually see the face of my Father in heaven. For the Son of man is come to save that which was lost."

(Matthew 18:10,11)

"All who make idols are nothing, and the things they delight in do not profit; their witnesses neither see nor know. And so they will be put to shame. Who would fashion a god or cast an image that can do no good?"

(Isaiah 44:9,10)

Rhythmic contractions of ancient forbears emanate through the genes of my Soul. They too, recognized the inflection in His voice. Listened for the sound of His footsteps near the icy waters edge. Exulted at His approach.

Saying, "Come Unto Me."
The Nations.
The powers and potentates.
The priests and religionists.
The doers and don'ts.
All continue their rituals of oblivion.
Each in his own way proclaiming:
"Messiah will never come!" They refuse to Dance. Authentic PRAYER is unknown to them. By temperment, they seem ill suited. By Life style, unworthy. Both are delusions. Hearing the VOICE of Jesus has distanced me from stereotypes, predispositions and the seduction of personality. (I have not always been here!) I am relieved to be here today. The time we spend on the planet must allow us to seek Beauty, herald JUSTICE, live generously and Dance to our heart's content.

The invitation of JESUS is for ALL the world to ***"Come"***
— out of delusion
— out of strife
— away from indecision
— beyond material ambition
— outside the church walls and into the kingdom of His LOVE.

This is Soul magic.
>A LOST—found
>BLIND—sighted
>Bound—liberated Reality.

To know this is to be "made whole." Perhaps, we all do. Perhaps, There is that moment when each of us is *really* aware of the pull *against* Divinity. In the congregations. The denominations. The ecumenical councils. And the monasteries. (Might the seeker also be pacifying an acute sense of rebellion in an attempt to privatize the Holy?") Those who have lost the way to prayer need dance lessons! Those who fear their own bodies need dance lessons! The one who cannot hear God must learn to Dance. LOVE CALLS. God is not dead. Each step requires a decision. Brings me closer to the moment of surrender. Invokes the POWER of His Presence. I have come to the edge of the LIVING WATERS. God's VOICE is like a Rainbow over hidden streams. TO PRAY, I must take the plunge. I must strip and let GO! I want to reach into eternity and pull up VISIONS of Development and PEACE for my people to share. I want to shake hands with the Angel of FOREVER. Drink from the cup of Providence. Sit with the Scribes of the Ages and eat at the "welcome table!"

But, this is the Sankofa Ballet. So there is always the magnetic pull of the unknown BEFORE.
Before THIS TIME.
BEFORE Conception.
BEFORE SIN.
BEFORE REJECTION.
BEFORE ASSIMILATION.
BEFORE COLONIALISM.
BEFORE LYNCHING.
BEFORE SHAME.
BEFORE CORRUPTION.
BEFORE "LET" . . . .

THREE

"Assuredly, I say to you, whatever you bind on earth will be bound in heaven, and whatever you loose on earth will be loosed in heaven."

(Matthew 18:18)

"As for you also, because of the blood of my covenant with you, I will set your prisoners free from the waterless pit. Return to your stronghold, O prisoners of hope; today I declare that I will restore to you double."

(Zechariah 9:11,12)

THREE

"O LORD, I have heard of your renown, and I stand in awe, O LORD, of your work. In our own time revive it; in our own time make it known; in wrath may you remember mercy."

(Habakkuk 3:2)

Before Oppression.
Before DECISION.
Before Miracles.
Before Consent.
Before LIGHT.
That undisclosed ocean of Eternity in which all secrets are hidden. That reluctant echo of a lost summer. To look back is not the uncontrolled urge of LOT's wife. It is the irresistible pull of a Soul mired in an anti-God culture. It is the courageous gesture of a Diaspora people with no memory of home. It is the defiant gaze of the one who can discern neither meaning nor beauty in this present hour. It is the Dance of Amazement.
LOOK what GOD has already done for me! How can I count the hours. The moments. The seconds in Eternity that are already mine?
Which way is Heaven?
Within.
Within.
I move in the flow of this gift called the Nile.
Allow the waters of remembering to wash over me.
Christ stands on the banks of the River.
Whispering to Nubian angels.
Now is as sweet as Forever.
FOREVER is made perfect in this moment.
Who can understand time?
Hold it in her hand?
Take its' wings and fly?
Time is a mystery. We are her gatekeepers.
Time is a mystery.

"Everything that is has already been!"
Time is a mystery.
The forgotten becomes the prophesied "not yet."
This is Sankofa.
Come Dance with me in the imagination of God.
"God's thoughts are not our thoughts."
So consider the magnitude of the force within God's imagination!
Colors.
Shapes
Histories.
Generations.
Sanctuaries.
An overture of apocalyptic proportions inhales and exhales the dancers themselves. A dramatic syncopation draws us into improbable realms of praying. GOD is NOT DEAD. God holds His breath as we wilt under the fire of His Presence. And then God breathes upon us the REFRESHING. The Past rises as the mist of a summer morning. All that remains is FOREVER. My Soul has been lubricated! I am seized by the Universe.
The incredible RADIANCE of Divinity. This is the LIGHT that will shine Forever.
This is the tempo of the Blessed.
Looking at life from the perspective of Eternity is a Peace enhancing experience. It is because of this, I now know that LIFE is illumined by our tragedies as well as our awakenings. In that Sacred moment when mortal breath is infused with Eternal Spirit; PRAYER HAPPENS. The realities of this encounter tutor the Soul.

THREE

"What has been is what will be, and what has been done is what will be done; there is nothing new under the sun."

(Ecclesiastes 1:9)

"Just as you do not know how the breath comes to the bones in the mother's womb, so you do not know the work of God, who makes everything."

(Ecclesiastes 11:5)

THREE

> *"We declare to you what was from the beginning, what we have heard, what we have seen with our eyes, what we have looked at and touched with our hands, concerning the word of life—"*
>
> *(1 John 1:1)*

Heaven is giddy over the union of what is and what has never been! Reluctant to spoil my entrance into the MYSTERY, I pause. My spiritual clumsiness must not be an affront to the sensitivities of Abba. I wait. Knowing the "urgency" is mine—not God's. I wait. In the SILENCE of the Holy ONE, I will trace His footprints with my heart. God's imaginings terrify the passive.

Exult the Soul.
Silence the vain.
and seal the Past.

> Let us declare this hour of beginnings.
> Re-enter the womb where the
> Zulu and the Ga are conceived.
>
> Create the scent of eucalyptus.
> The feel of aloe.
> The sound of the dolphin.
> and the color of chartreuse.
> Let us see for the first time
> the LIGHT of the world.

I recognize **JESUS**,
> He is "wrapped in swaddling
> clothes" laying unclaimed in a
> nursery for children born with aids.

I recognize **JESUS**,
> He is curled up in a refugee camp
> dying of dysentery, cholera and
> other curable diseases.

I recognize **JESUS**.

She is about to give birth to her first child under a bridge in Manhattan.

I recognize **JESUS**.
>   On line at the unemployment office.
>   Assignment: GOLGOTHA

No small gift, this Calvary. This redemption. This Cosmic intricacy for new beginnings. I am certain of my future because my past begins here. My personal particular past. My collective identity past and my KINGDOM inheritance. All here. The Past that begins Eternity for me.

"Those who live at earth's farthest bounds are awed by your signs; you make the gateways of the morning and the evening shout for joy." (Psalms 65:8)

From this corner of Eternity, I behold the splendor of a HOPE too real to be denied. A restoration immune to human sabotage. A grand chorale in Doxologies that bring oppressors to repentance.
Humanity is caught up in an effortless crescendo of PRAISE. These are the Songs of the disinherited. The forgotten. The overlooked. Until the SHINING of the LIGHT.

Now let the dancing church emerge to rule over the nations.
God shall not dance alone!
Creation will not be unaccompanied.
The Souls of Believers EVERYWHERE in EVERY Generation shall be "loosed" to DANCE.
>   This is "HIGH" Prayer.
>   Holy Prayer.
>   Prayer without Boundaries.
>   This is "low" prayer.
>   Holy Prayer.

THREE

"After this I saw four angels standing at the four corners of the earth, holding back the four winds of the earth so that no wind could blow on earth or sea or against any tree. I saw another angel ascending from the rising of the sun, having the seal of the living God, and he called with a loud voice to the four angels who had been given power to damage earth and sea,"

(Revelation 7:1,2)

THREE

> Prayer without manuscript.
> This is Eucharistic Prayer.
> Deliverance Prayer.
> Baptismal Prayer.
> Every bit Pentecostal Prayer!
> Prayer prayed without Merit or Means.
> Prayer prayed with motion and language.
> Prayer prayed and heard.
> Prayer heard and Answered.
> PRAYER answered and Confirmed.

The past can no longer be a reproach or a deterrent.
The LIGHT is shining.
All God's secrets are being revealed.
Idea is being dwarfed by wonder!
The PASSION of God's forgiveness thrills the hearts of those of us who just couldn't seem to get it right. And a quiet flame of Holiness is ignited in our souls.
We now understand GRACE and MERCY.
The LIGHT is Shining.
"The past belongs to God." It sings.
The cadence is one of STRENGTH and PROMISE.
"The PAST belongs to God."
The LIGHT shines and sings.
   Sings and shines.
   Shines and Sings.
This LIGHT is shining in my SOUL.
This LIGHT is shining in my SOUL.

THREE

At this moment; if there be any GUILT.
        if there by any ECSTASY.
        if there by any Uncertainty or
        unexpressed DESIRE—
Let me now BEHOLD it.
Give thanks for the life lessons it teaches.
Embrace mySelf.
SIT in the Presence of the LOVE of GOD for a Season.
ARISE and LIVE.

    Dear Cojourner,
This is by no means a modest undertaking.
The bare Essentials of Prayer for the hurting heart are a SIGH. A TEAR. A DESIRE FOR GOD. It is helpful to take an intercessor/Counselor/SPIRITUAL DIRECTOR/THERAPIST with you, when you pray into your PAST. This is HEALING GROUND. The GATEWAY TO A New FUTURE. SHILOH!
    Relax your Body.
    Listen to your Body.
    Allow your Body to express YOU.
    Let every cell in your Body whisper to GOD.
    GOD will respond.
    You will know it in your body.
See the changes in your body—your hair, sight, walk, weight, teeth ... See and LISTEN. You are the perfect, unique manifestation of your past.

                SELAH

THREE

"And the Word became flesh and lived among us, and we have seen his glory, the glory as of a father's only son, full of grace and truth."

(John 1:14)

RITES of PASSAGE

Albeit, there is a certain solemnity due the consideration of antiquities.
So I will bow my head.
Lower my gaze.
Maintain an appropriate sense of reverence.
Avoid extravagant gestures.
Remain SILENT.
And pass on to the FUTURE!
This is one of the beauties of PRAYER.
The reality of PASSAGE.
From one time to another.
From one condition to another.
From one Mercy to another.
Yet there is only ONE LIGHT.
THE TRUE LIGHT.
And I am a Reflection of that LIGHT.

I have seen the LIGHT.
My SOUL is hungry for the LIGHT.
Healed by the LIGHT.
Strengthened by the LIGHT.
This LIGHT is JESUS.
He is the reason I pray.
> I dance.
> I shout.
> I fly.

This LIGHT guides me through the past into the present and Forward to Eternity. The Cojourner passes from creation to Conversion to Confession to Covenant to Consecration. Each a matter of Kairos—the "fullness of TIME." It is a matter of one's PRAYER LIFE—I am moved from GOD, to GOD, for GOD, with GOD, in GOD! These five Grace encounters—RITES of Passage—connote the intensity of SPIRITUAL awareness and acumen. Again, let the Cojourner search her past to learn their origins, meaning and direction. To know the path of her Spiritual Journey. To give voice to her authentic prayer.

There is no way to anticipate the mood of prayer. No way of knowing which way the SOUL will respond to the moment. No way of intuiting what GOD has in mind when the SPIRIT begins to groan and to genuflect. The body is present to this ENCOUNTER of the mundane with the primordial. Yet the body itself becomes transparent. This is due to the supernatural energies that accompany PRAYER. Consider the mystery of it. No matter how long I do so, the unknown still remains greater than that which is KNOWN. PRAYER keeps its own secrets! Haunts our waking and sleeping consciousness.
Tintillates our imaginations.
Waits for no one.
A vow to pray is no modest proposition.
It is God's integrity that is being wagered.
In the sanctuaries, more often than not, the prayers are orchestrated to elicit a response *from* the people. God's involvement is coincidental. Yet, too, in those same sanctuaries there can be a superior engagement of the human and the Holy. When the Souls of the people become the concourse of the Heavenlies. At such times as this, we learn that there is music in PRAYER.
Silent.
Sensory.
Evocative.
Compelling.
Invading.
This music rummages through all my superficial belongings and discards them without a hint of apology. This music calls me to a new awareness. It is the prelude to a Dance that will transform my Soul.

THREE

"When he did come out, he could not speak to them, and they realized that he had seen a vision in the sanctuary. He kept motioning to them and remained unable to speak."

(Luke 1:22)

THREE

To my CoJourner:

As you pursue DEPTH LISTENING *of what is now being offered; become the "speaker" and let your heart experience transformation:*

SOLILOQUY OF A LOST—FOUND DANCER

It may as well be MIDNIGHT.
I am cautious.
    shy.
    intimidated.
    eager.
    excited.
    fearful.
    needy.
    delighted,
(over dressed I'm sure!)

There are others here.
They have so much to recommend them.
(they are dressed properly)
They come offering bouquets of song.
They stand on the approval of the elders.
Their obedience is sterling.
Sacrifices consistent.
Families well-ordered.

"HE will NEVER choose me!"

They pray with humility.
They are in submission to authority.
They give honor to the men.

They don't call attention to themselves

THREE

"He will NEVER choose me!"

I blurt out my needs without appropriate greetings.
I always forget protocol.
Scowl with anger when I am hurt.
Despise the Saints.
Defy my husband.
Ignore the liturgy.

"He will *never* choose me!"

Even so, I want to Dance with GOD.
I want to leap into GOD's embrace and
    swoon under the Power of God's leading.
I want to say with my Body
What language cannot utter.
I want to be draped in the Cloak of Heaven,
be chaperoned by the Angels.
And have the STARS
blush with envy.
I want to waltz with God through
the corridors of infirmity
and have the sick
RISE healed from their beds.
With my head resting on God's heart,
I want to learn the LOVE song of the
DIVINE.

THREE

                    "Choose me Abba,
                            choose me . . .

My hips were shaped in the Congo.
My head raised like the Senegaleze.
My forehead regal as the Ashanti.
My shoulders broad as the Bassa.
My back strong as the Masai.
My legs firm as Palm Trees.
My arms glistering as the Mende.

                    "Choose me Abba,
                            choose me . . ."

My heart is as courageous as thunder.
My desire as intense as the Rain forest.
My gait as sure as the lioness.
My sight as keen as the owl.
My fidelity as strong as the elephant.
My need as vast as the ocean.
My song as penetrating as 1,000 drums.

                    "Choose me Abba,
                            choose me . . ."

Preparing for the Dance, my heart is reckless.
My ZEAL out of control.
My imagination relentless.
Reason exhausts itself trying to catch up—
and finally surrenders.

The music is within me.
Panasonic.
Penetrating.
Orchestral.
Tintillating.

I am Electric.
    Ecstatic.
Immersed in Holy Hymnody.
Ready to Expire!

THREE

Messiah enters the place.
There is a frenzy of desire throughout.
I withdraw to my familiar corner of rejection.
Silence my longing.
Stain my robe with tears of mud.

Suddenly the LIGHT shines.
It is upon me!
      about me!
         WITHIN me!

"I am my Beloved's
   and my Beloved
      is mine"
           [Song of Solomon 2:16]

My feet touch the sky.
My heart illumines the NATIONS.
My JOY fills Eternity with song.

    "He chose ME,
        He chose ME.
    He chose ME."

   God and I Dance in the midst of the Universe. I Dance with GOD in the presence of Angels. GOD Dances with me to bring Hope to the Church. This HOLY DANCE is for the Healing of the NATIONS.

           "HE CHOSE ME."

God chose me.
REJECTION is a delusion.
Isolation, a mirage.
Fear, an empty shadow.
I was born for GOD.
In GOD I LIVE.
And now, I DANCE with GOD.
FOREVER.
Amen.

THREE

THE POWER OF SOUL

Sankofa meanings unravel as the well-worn Garment of struggle is discarded. The garment being woven for me now is the "garment of PRAISE." Threads of Pain from my Past are intricately woven with those of deliverance, art and countless epiphanies. *Illumination* is the weaver. An artisan of greater skill and dexterity than **dread**. In the former days, it was dread that clothed me.

The Altar of GOD is no place for dread. Some were dancing there who moved to the cadence of Death. A slow persistent thud. Heavy with a lifetime of disappointment:
- childhood gone too soon
- sorrow that stayed too long
- no night seasons of ecstasy to remember
- no prayer life to mention
- no Holy icons to recall the Vision
- no will to fight on anymore

So blinded by their own thick sadness, they cannot see that they are naked, nimble, redeemed and ALIVE. They invoke a peace that will never come. The Judas choreographer has hindered their thoughts and their bodies obey. Halt. Crippled. Handicapped. BOUND. A slow persistent thud. Heavy with despair. Weighed down with memories of PAIN. They cannot hear the music of Prayer. Their bodies no longer sing. Their hearts refuse to Pray. I will not remain among them. My soul longs to dance. My soul has a memory of life with God.

My SOUL has the capacity to retrieve my mind, my body, my heart, and my desire from the trenches of dread. MY SOUL won't let me die. Won't let me waste away to purposeless living. MY SOUL is intent on my Rising from this chaos, this lethargy, this neurosis. MY SOUL is greater than *my* memory of mySelf. More powerful than the accusations that have been leveled against me by myself or others. MY SOUL is the source and Reservoir of TRUTH in my life. My Soul is *still* the LIVING SPACE of God in *my* body.

I will listen to my Soul. I will exit this ensemble of dread. I will pray for the baptism of the Spirit of Prayer. I will allow my heart to express the voiceless, wordless, agonizing, motionless meaning of my plight.
Incomplete thoughts.
Broken verbs.
Pronoun-less identities.
Garble.
Ramblings.
SIGHTS.
God will hear.
God will know.
God is not DEAD.

   Now I understand why PRAYER and DANCE can be synonyms. Both engage the whole person-Spirit and body, memory and expectation, passion and Reason. Both are the expression of inward promptings. Each allows the seeker the highest form of Communication. SOUL VOICE. The message moves through me. The meaning is a burning flame within me. This WORD has power. This power has me. This woman must Dance!

Can I live, if I do not PRAY?
Is it really PRAYER, if I refuse to
       DANCE?
         What is this aching?
         This tension?
         This aimless grieving?
Surely it is the accumulation of aborted PRAYERS!

THREE

"There is no speech, nor are there words; their voice is not heard; yet their voice goes out through all the earth, and their words to the end of the world. In the heavens he has set a tent for the sun,"

(Psalms 19:3,4)

"Fools say in their hearts, "There is no God." They are corrupt, they commit abominable acts; there is no one who does good."

(Psalms 53:1)

"Be gracious to me, O LORD, for I am languishing; O LORD, heal me, for my bones are shaking with terror. My soul also is struck with terror, while you, O LORD—how long?"

(Psalms 6:2,3)

THREE

A Life of HOLINESS is **not** as readily available as the desire itself. Although the LIFE must spring from the desire. Desire is tenuous.
It wilts and surges.
    fades and crumbles.
    soars and disappears.

And then, without warning, DESIRE mounts to unbridled heights. The inner world of the Soul is a mystery. There is magic in the Mystery. The Soul is intrigued by its own Passion. It is not unlikely, that in your pursuit of God you will exhaust ALL DESIRE.
        Grow Faint.
        Become Weary.
          Empty.
          Drained.

A Paradox of the Oblate life is what we experience as
   the death of DESIRE.
It is crucified by bad, meaningless religion.
It is buried in the foolishness of the culture and the
   absurdities of personal distractions.
Desire is DEAD.
    Goes down to the grave.
    Emaciated.
    Forlorn.
    Lifeless.
        DEAD.
Without benefit of
ceremony, mourners or pall
bearers; Desire is buried.
        Dead without NOTICE.

Yet, some how rises! More profound. More intense. More determined. When the DESIRE for Holiness takes on its own REALITY, the LIFE will soon follow. Until now, I have danced **for** GOD. But my deep DESIRE is to dance **with** GOD. A longing born of too many years dancing alone. And too many years standing still—not dancing at all! Protocol, Anger, Unforgiveness, Fear—had silenced my authentic voice—my Dance.

    I did not realize God wanted to Dance with me! I never knew that this Dance; this life of Prayer; this call to Holiness; was God's own Gift to me. To bless me and protect me. To encourage me and keep me strong. To bring me JOY and laughter and Song. To keep me out of the clutches of the evil one. I just didn't know. **SELAH**.

    Let me now gather the fragments of my past.
        Unreconciled?
        Undeserved?
        Unrecycled?
        Unyielding?

Be that as it may; I will put them in a crystal basket, dance with them to the Altar of Release and LEAVE them there. I know I have a Higher Past. A past where fear is fused with miracles. A Past where Beauty is uncensored. Holidays exhilarating. When my heart, like 5th Avenue was open to throngs of extravagant shoppers. When God came without invocations and rocked me in a Mississippi hotel,
        Stretched out over me on a Cambridge floor
          burst out in LIGHT above me at the
              top of a Yonkers stairwell
        Angeled me on a transAtlantic flight
        and wrote to me in a Nigerian guest house.

When I open the window of my Past,
I see neighbors coming to help when the house was on fire.
I see a father who worked until he couldn't work anymore.
I see William Luther Wallace standing in the gap.
I see a friend giving me half her sandwich because
    I didn't have any.
I see the dignity of the POOR!
I see those compassionate although wealthy.
I SEE GOD.

THREE

"I have seen their ways, but I will heal them; I will lead them and repay them with comfort, creating for their mourners the fruit of the lips."

(Isaiah 57:18)

"The joy of our hearts has ceased; our dancing has been turned to mourning."

(Lamentations 5:15)

"when at midday along the road, your Excellency, I saw a light from heaven, brighter than the sun, shining around me and my companions."

(Acts 26:13)

THREE

"Sing aloud, O daughter Zion; shout, O Israel! Rejoice and exult with all your heart, O daughter of Jerusalem! The LORD has taken away the judgments against you, he has turned away your enemies. The king of Israel, the LORD, is in your midst; you shall fear disaster no more. On that day it shall be said to Jerusalem: Do not fear, O Zion; do not let your hands grow weak. The LORD, your God, is in your midst, a warrior who gives victory; he will rejoice over you with gladness, he will renew you in his love; he will exult over you with loud singing as on a day of festival. I will remove disaster from you, so that you will not bear reproach for it. I will deal with all your oppressors at that time. And I will save the lame and gather the outcast, and I will change their shame into praise and renown in all the earth. At that time I will bring you home, at the time when I gather you; for I will make you renowned and praised among all the peoples of the earth, when I restore your fortunes before your eyes, says the LORD."

(Zephaniah 3:14–20)

These epiphanies unleash a torrent of pirouettes in my soul. Cool the fevers of depression. Create orgiastic tremors throughout my body. Slap death! And I am made whole by that which I had **forgotten**.

The Past need not be a door sealed closed. Marked "DO NOT ENTER." A dungeon of foreboding. Finding my way there is helping me to progress! Rosary beads include the realities of our Past: CHRIST born. CHRIST suffering. CHRIST RISEN from the dead. The Praying heart brings these recollections into her present experience. The Past is both gone *and* with us. It is what points us to the outskirts of mortality. The Past is unique, particular, unduplicated. An x-ray of the Soul, a photograph of the mind, a census of the body—will reveal that it is ever Present. With the Holy Spirit as my chaperone, I come home to my personal particular past.

Embrace.
Pause.
and waltz into Forever.

Dear Cojourner,

Flight from the PAST, often means abandoning a whole garden just to avoid a few weeds! The Past has many messages which may very well shape my DESTINY.

I FREE my Past from the language of blame and SELF JUSTIFICATION. The healthy roots of a future are there. This is the reservoir of my Soul.

With your body, express what it means to REACH INTO your Past; to give thanks for your Past;
to Release your Past into the arms of ETERNITY.
NOW LET US DANCE . . .

Search the Psalms to find that word
                              or verse
                              or passage
that will escort you into your PAST.

SANKOFA brings the awareness of the past as "GIFT." Sankofa teaches me to retrieve the light from dark and shadowy places. SANKOFA offers balance to a life too overwhelmed by the PRESENT; TOO CONSUMED WITH THE FUTURE and/or TOO DISTRACTED by illusions of the PAST.

To my Cojourner:

> *The scriptures teach that the "Holy Spirit will recall that which I must know."*
>
> ***Today****, by the GRACE of GOD,*
>   *I am given the GIFT of a <u>beautiful</u> personal past:*
> *Great benefit will come.*
>   *Let us write "what the Spirit says."*
>
> **At THIS very moment in this SPACE!**

THREE

"But the Advocate, the Holy Spirit, whom the Father will send in my name, will teach you everything, and remind you of all that I have said to you."

(John 14:26)

"saying, Write in a book what you see and send it to the seven churches"

(Revelation 1:11a)

AMEN.

THREE

On the next three pages are PRAYERS of REMEMBERING. My prayer to GOD for you is that by the POWER of the Holy Spirit, you will be helped to
- RECLAIM precious moments
- RE-understand painful experiences
- RE-connect with persons you may have forgotten or taken for granted
- RE-ENTER beautiful spaces and most of all to
- RE-IMAGINE yourself in the world!

FREE yourself to actually "WRITE" what you receive/ EXPERIENCE in the SPIRIT. Don't be intimidated by form or spelling or grammar.
- RELIVE
- RE-WORD
- RELEASE

your living Past.
- GIVE yourself TIME.
- Stretch or
- Do some deep breathing exercises before you begin.

Have FAITH that healing will come!

PRAYERS OF REMEMBERING   THREE

    LORD Jesus Christ.
    God of my beginnings.
    Make alive for me
    in my Spirit mind
    the occasions when
    I was blessed; but did not know it.
    Show me the unclaimed treasures
    of Your Mercy.
                Selah.

"WRITE WHAT THE SPIRIT SAYS."

    "I will bless the LORD
    at all times.
    His praise shall continually
    be in my mouth." (Psalms 34:1)

          * * * * * * *

THREE

Holy WORD.
Recall the conversations,
the remarks, the gestures
of affection that poured
out to me from a
genuine, caring Soul.
                        Selah.

"WRITE WHAT THE SPIRIT SAYS."

"I will bless the LORD
at all times.
His praise shall continually
be in my mouth." (Psalms 34:1)

             * * * * * * *

Sweet VISITATION.　　　　　　　　　　　**THREE**
Descend upon my memory
with images of those
who have been kind to me,
generous,
patient,
forgiving,
encouraging . . .
with no ulterior motive.
　　　　　　　　Selah.

"WRITE WHAT THE SPIRIT SAYS."

　　　　"I will bless the LORD
　　　　at all times.
　　　　His praise shall continually
　　　　be in my mouth." (Psalms 34:1)

　　　　　　　* * * * * * *

THREE

The "silenced" prophet is never a "silent" prophet.
Dead or ALIVE—she speaks!
> In the pulpit.
> In the pew.
> In the marketplace.
> In the shadows.
> In the LIGHT.

The Past is in her womb. The future, in her bosom. Today is in her heart. She will never be denied. "The Glory of the LORD is risen upon her." She has nothing to fear of the Past. Nothing in her future has the POWER to destroy her. Today, her thoughts are clear. GOD will not "rest" until her word is spoken.
> Vision revealed.
> Hope ignited.

The Past is *A* reality *in* GOD. LET IT COME!
The moon over my past is GLORY.
The moon over my past is indigo joy.
The moon over my past is star-washed rain.
The moon over my past is framed in a rainbow.
The moon over my past rides on the back of the Lion of Judah.
LET HIM COME.
> The prophet awaits.
> The nations tremble.
> The ceilings have been torn off the churches!

It is here.
The Past is undeniably Ascent.

> Selah.

The Dance of Return is done to the Rhythm of the KINGDOM. God reminds the chosen. The very ONENESS and Wonder of GOD defy time-space limitations. Consequently, Prayers of Remembrance open us to a "NEW" Past and a Greater DESTINY! The Oblate who walks in a prophetic anointing, has a call unlike any other. She *sees* into the heart of things natural and things spiritual. She gives GOD "NO REST" and the people no escape. The KINGDOM is everything. She must Dance boldly; even when her movements are hidden from syncretists,
>> cowards,
>> hypocrits and
>> oppressors.

The Spirit that roared in the Soul Life of NZINGA, now rises in the sleepless dreams of NZINGA's daughters. Their prophetic presence calls out repression in the emotion of soulless clerics. But it is too late! Too late! Much too Late! The Dance has begun. The Spirit of Prophecy is moving in the midst of the Nations. The prophet calls God to remembrance as well as the people.

To be able to declare, "I remember" is a powerful and liberating experience! To remember is to focus. To prevail. To acknowledge. To remember brings momentum and clairty to the life of faith. To be "UN-remembered" creates a sense of humiliation and tragic anonymity!

God is continually calling Israel to remembrance—"I am the LORD your GOD, who brought you OUT . . ." (Leviticus 25:55)
"Remember the Sabbath day, to keep it Holy . . " (Ex. 20:8)
"This do in remembrance of me . . ." (Luke 22:19)
Remembrance is what maintains the life flow—for the Oblate, for a people and for the NATIONS. What is LIFE without "memory?"

Life without memory is incomplete.
>> inauthentic.
>> incoherent!

THREE

"Remember His marvelous works which He has done, His wonders, and the judgements of His mouth,"
(Psalm 105:5)

"You who make mention of the LORD, do not keep silent, and give Him no rest . . ."
(Isaiah 62:6b–79)

"If I forget thee, O Jerusalem, may my right hand lose its' cunning."
(Psalm ???)

THREE

The Past has both properties of chastisement and encouragement. The unclaimed "Before;" the unknown "Before"; and the unmanifested "BEFORE" are as much mine as the present moment. Somehow, the Dance of Return "strengthens feeble knees." It makes the heart healthy. Inspires the Soul. Clarifies Sight. Enlightens the mind. The Dance of Return is done in concentric circles: my personal particular past, my Collective Identify past and my Kingdom past. Each has its own unique cadence yet heightens the impact of the other two.

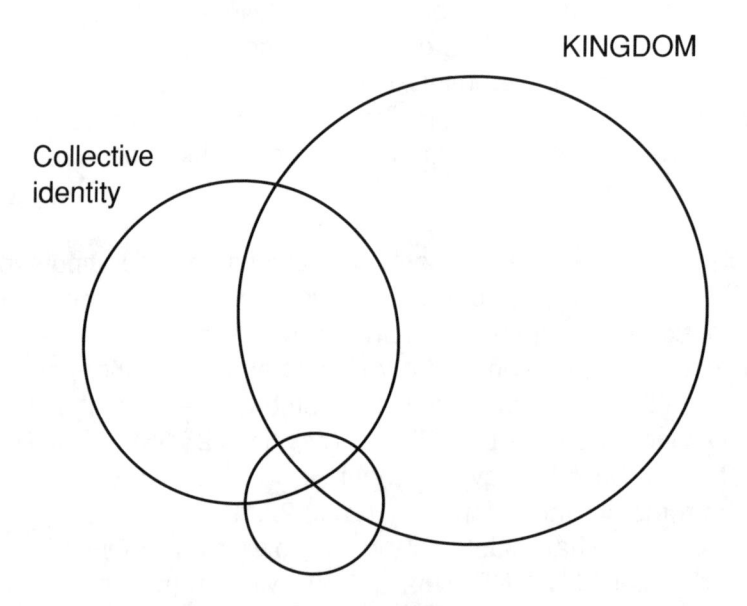

THREE

These are the worlds within which I explore my Spiritual meaning and Purpose. These are my realms of origin. Daily I am discovered by some treasure of my own antiquity. The ruminations of my past often gather for a pre-dawn raid into my consciousness. And I awaken with the profound sense of having lived there Again! I remember and I Dance.

This must be the meaning of Sankofa to the Ashanti of West Africa and the "New World"—"go back to go forward."

There is such force of SPIRIT
    such Power of Soul
        such FORTITUDE of memory in my Collective Identify Past, that I cannot but glory in it! I discern the Supernatural meaning of the sufferings of my people. It is the Messianic burden. The Christ Covenant. I explore the chronicles of our oppression. And when I get over the feelings of being angry, hurt, frightened and abandoned by God—I am charmed by the sheer majesty of our Self renewal.

SANKOFA.
Go Back and be Healed.
SANKOFA.
Go Back and Conquer.
SANKOFA.
Go Back and LISTEN.
SANKOFA.
Go Back and RELEASE. FORGIVE. LET GO.
SANKOFA.
Go Back and COME BACK!

THREE

Once I leave this "cleft" in the ROCK, I can only go FORWARD. What I have seen will never be as powerful as that which remains unseen. But it is more than enough! The Past was never intended to bind. It is to edify. The Past teaches me about GOD. It speaks of the Egyptian flight, the controversy in the temple, the transfiguration and Legion in the vernacular of my own experiences! And I learn something more about GOD. Something irrefutable. Beyond doubt. LIBERATING. The Past is not my enemy. It is my tutor.

Jesus, Himself, asks to be remembered—BROUGHT FORWARD!

> "As often as you can,
> do THIS in Remembrance
> of me." (Luke 22:19)

The Past has the capacity to make the Present come ALIVE in ways that nothing else can. The Streams of Eternity flow backward and FORWARD carrying the VISION of the Kingdom for each generation forever. I am not imprisoned in this spot. I am in concert with a dynamic continuity. I am *not* constrained by the Present moment or circumstances as known by chronological dimensions. I am as the widow preparing to die until Elijah comes! I am as Job horrified and condemned until GOD came in person. I am like Mary, walking around with a miracle in my belly that the world is not ready to receive. The Past is my assurance. My evidence. My buffer against annihilation. The Past is my friend.

So let me Dance.
Let me answer "THE CALL" with Dignity, Courage, and Grace. I will Dance with Total sensitivity to the Presence of GOD in my life. A "friendly" Past walks not far from every abusive, annoying or disappointing PAST. GOD is in my PAST. GLORY is in my PAST. That is what makes me an ARTIST in the medium of the Spiritual. For some it is clay or fabric or the Camera or music. OR, You name it. But as for me, my creativity is expressed in the SPIRIT. I am an ARTIST.

I understand that now! Only after long years of ignorance. FEAR, ANGER, BITTERNESS—these three.
ANGER, BITTERNESS, FEAR—soaked in religious excuses.
BITTERNESS, FEAR, ANGER—cost me days of song, my good health, and the capacity for meaningful relationships.

The spell is broken. The "reproach has been removed."
    "take away from me their scorn and contempt,
        for I have kept your decrees."
                      (Psalms 119:22)

    ". . . you anoint my head with oil;
        my cup overflows."
                      (Psalms 23:5b)

The Past is a "wind song." Between midnight and morning she descends. At times with a eulogistic aura. Often as a sequel to the present. Frequently, the Past shows up on her own. Unsolicited, Unwelcome. Inappropriate. I have learned to rise and greet her as a friendly or unfriendly passer by. When she brings beauty, inspiration or Light; I invite her to Dance with me for awhile. Just so that I can know again the TOUCH, the flow, the power, the insight of the HOLY from days now gone. Seasons unremembered. I want to hear again the eloquence of youthful naivete and the sombre prose of passion's indiscretion.

    My life is not over. It begins anew with every healing remembrance. You see, in the Spirit realm, I am perpetually born again and again and again! There is magic in this Dance. To throw my head back while sending my feet forward. To launch and return in the same movement.
    This body is a miracle.
This body is the friend of prayer.
A true and loving friendship it must always be.

THREE

"Blessed be the LORD, for he has wondrously shown his steadfast love to me when I was beset as a city under siege. I had said in my alarm, "I am driven far from your sight." But you heard my supplications when I cried out to you for help."
                      (Psalms 31:21,22)

"Look at the nations, and see! Be astonished! Be astounded! For a work is being done in your days that you would not believe if you were told."
                      (Habakkuk 1:5)

THREE

"We have escaped like a bird from the snare of the fowlers; the snare is broken, and we have escaped. Our help is in the name of the LORD, who made heaven and earth."

(Psalms 124:8)

"Thus says the LORD, the Redeemer of Israel and his Holy One, to one deeply despised, abhorred by the nations, the slave of rulers, "Kings shall see and stand up, princes, and they shall prostrate themselves, because of the LORD, who is faithful, the Holy One of Israel, who has chosen you."

(Isaiah 49:7)

There are other midnights, however, when the chilly wind of the past surrounds me with the luminous shadows of failure, the unforgiven dead, and doors that I have refused to enter. My body grows cold, stiff, frigid. I will not accept *this* Dance. I will follow the Holy power within me. I will lay down beneath the cross of JESUS CHRIST. And my body and my Spirit will echo to each other the Reality of Jesus in my life. The Song of the Wind will be transformed from shame to deliverance. And I will recite in my heart the many times God has brought me out of affliction, oppression, persecution and a Hellish Fear too ominous to be ignored.

My vocation is PRAYER. In prayer I am united with humanity and Divinity. To LIVE to PRAY is my heart's fondest desire. The history of the nations justifies a life of prayer.

The frailty of the churches; the discouragement of the women; the ethos of death; mandate a covenant of Prayer. To intercede for those whom God will judge as Moses did for Miriam. To take the initiative for leadership as Deborah did. To wait for a pentecost as the disciples and the women did.

By the POWER of Prayer, my life shall become bread for the poor, learning for the untutored and SILENCE for chaos. I want to pray NOT out of "fear" or "necessity" but because of my ardent desire for God's love to reign in the world. I am dissuaded from ambition by the summons to humility. This is an on-going struggle. Humility is not something to be learned in the culture or in the churches for that matter! Only the Spirit of the LORD can counsel me on this issue.

Write an affirmation that will nurture the Spirit of humility in your life:

PRAYER for me is not "compulsion," it is LIFE and breath itself. I believe that I am here on this planet as an expression of the Perfecting POWER of PRAYER. I allow the MYSTERY to breathe, unmolested by my emotion. And my thoughts become the music of GOD to the Universe because I have surrendered my faculties to the Holy SPIRIT. This is the WONDER of Prayer. It is so much easier NOW to be awakened by the boundless Reality of the Eternal; to reflect the Shekinah Glory of God. PRAYER draws me into the flow of GOD's majestic promenade through time. I hold hands with infinity. There is music *and* LIGHT in my Body. For I have become a LIVING Soul. And I Dance with GOD.

To know Sankofa, consider a pregnant woman. The past, the present and the future are wrapped in one body. This is the Church, Queen of the Dance. Over-shadowed by the Holy Spirit, she has conceived the New Day, the New Generation, the New Vision. Daily she goes back to Calvary and the tomb. Daily she brings the future nigh! It is of her that the Scripture speaks when it says, "The Spirit *and* the Bride say come."

Write an affirmation of your PAST:

THREE

"I consider that the sufferings of this present time are not worth comparing with the glory about to be revealed to us."

(Romans 8:18)

". . . I was not disobedient to the vision from heaven."

(Acts 26:19)

THREE

INTERLUDE

"Your Kingdom is an everlasting kingdom, and your dominion endures through all generations. The Lord is faithful to all his promises and loving toward all he has made." (Psalm 145:13)

I give my body to this Psalm. There is such a tremendous REALITY in the message therein. I cannot escape the desire to peer into the faces of the Angels as I Dance this Dance. It is something to pray toward. This Dance anticipates the moment when all peoples and nations and tongues will join together in worshipping the LORD. Imagine. Imagine. An outpouring of Doxological LOVE so strong, so pure, so Divine—it permeates the Universe. As we prepare to cross over into Forever, we are assured, that this is the one time there will be no need to look back!

SANKOFA.
Having looked back, I go forward to:
-
-
-
-
-

INTERLUDE THREE

The Dancer Opens the Universe to the POWER of GOD. The universe welcomes the Presence of GOD with Dancing.

Tall trees
dusty roads
shattered glass
wandering cows
fidgety third graders
church janitors
Silent Madonnas

become beauty raptured when the Spirit of Prophecy goes forth. The artist lives in anticipation of this moment. The moment when, having Encountered the LIGHT of GOD, inner Space is created for an expanded Soul Life. When there is not enough "SPACE" on the inside to dream, to imagine, to feel deeply, to see, to ponder, to relanguage; the Soul is handicapped. What/who is occupying your creative SPACE? Every gift MUST breathe, genuflect, STRETCH and SHINE. PRAY *IN* your Gift. In the Dark. On Sunlit mornings. On the TRAIN. In the AIR. Wherever possible. Experience the Universe hugging you back. REST *in* your Gift. PRAYER is REALITY. Prayer is life. I once knew a woman who served meals that tasted as though they had been prepared *for* GOD. I learned that she prayed over each of the ingredients. She prayed throughout the entire cooking process. She prayed as she served the food. Surely, the Spirit of the LORD having been so faithfully and lovingly invoked; prevailed in Blessing the palate and life of everyone who sat at that table! Each of us has been offered the Universe in which to contemplate

create
vision
wander
gaze

and sup with GOD.

Your gift is the shortest and surest way to GOD. It is the splendor of the heavenlies in our journey through mortality. We worship a dancing GOD! One whose movements and rhythmns span the ages. A GOD whose Self-Consciousness is not defeated by Unbelief. This GOD who returns to us in the simplicity of bread and wine; the anguish of crucifixion; and the mystery of incarnation. This GOD, who in the Power of

"Behold, I stand at the door and knock. If anyone hears my voice, I will come in and sup with them."

(Rev. 3:20)

THREE

His Resurrection poured out Gifts upon humanity as He ascended.
(Ephesians 4:7,8)
Now opens Himself to us to receive our offerings.
Breathes into our Souls Kingdom imaginings.
Taps the shoulder of our memory with oceanic healing.
Provokes us to leave our water jars. (John 4:28)
And invites us to step out of the boat of the ordinary.
(Matthew 14:29–31)
Now that you have, this is your moment in Eternity;
What will You do with it?
                    SELAH

DANCE OF THE UNSPOKEN

SILENCE FEELS LIKE:

FOUR

There is a quiet center that breathes health into my Soul. A still and quiet place that loves me into authentic Reality. There are no shadows here. No illusions. It is here that I receive the POWER to BE.
    To BE OPEN.
    To BE in harmony.
    To BE fully human.
        FULLY ALIVE.
            Aware.
            Reflective.

I pray to enter this Quiet Center. And then I pray until that "center" becomes the Whole. This is for me and for many a "self"-conscious disciplining of the Spirit. I take myself away from the noise of my own life issues. Not merely the physical "to dos." That's the easy part. But to turn my whole mind toward the Presence of GOD. To disengage my emotions from the unreconciled controversies of my past and the deluge of uncertainties that brood over my present—this is a challenge! So much of this is the terrifying stuff of relationships:
    female—male
    female—female
    family
    Ministry
    Covenant Council

The energy involved is exhausting! There are no assurances. There is only the WIND. The Storm. The Calm. And the Sea. "Study to be QUIET" (I Thess. 4:11), the Scripture says. For only then can you "abound more and more." (I Thess. 4:1)

    "Lord, lead me to
    that Quiet
    Center.
    Where I can
    hear the Music
    of my own Soul.
    Where I can
    drink the Pure
    waters of
    Revelation.
    Where I can
    be Healed
    of ALL
    my diseases."
        Amen.

FOUR

And the LORD said,
  "Deny yourSelf,
  Take up you Cross
  and follow me." (Mathew 16:24)

Lord, who have I been following?
and Where am I now?

"Deny Yourself."

If I Let go, will my world fall apart?

"Yes."

Can I live in a broken dream?

"No. But you can make your Home in me!"

How LORD?

"Deny Yourself.
And BE MADE WHOLE."

    SELAH.

I will "study to be quiet." It is *in* me to BE so. There is a quiet room in my heart. I will go there and wait *quietly* for GOD to SPEAK. "Quiet" is medicine. "Quiet" is a song. "Quiet" is the signature of GOD. The more I "deny" mySelf, the quieter I become. It is time now to pursue the meanings of this discipline. To experience the benefits of it. To explore the unfamiliar terrain of my own Soul Life. I will search for WISDOM in "Quiet" places. Plant a garden of HOPE there. REST in the Spirit. "Quiet" is the medicine of the Universe. "Quiet" is the ancestor of Miracles.

"Quiet" asks its' own questions.
Does not require an answer.
Drinks from the Well of GOD.
"Quiet" is the vow that the snow makes to the Earth.
                      The bud to the branch.
                      And clouds to the sky.
These are the teachers of my Soul. The exemplars of Spirit dance. They are the embodiment of rhythmn and the unknown. "Quiet" is an untitled Sacrament.

To My CoJourner: FOUR

>How many times has your heart stood
>   still and you could not speak?
>Was there ever a moment of such
>amazement
>pain
>sorrow or
>exhiliration
>that your mind could shape no thought in response?
>When your Soul is so empty of breath that all you
>   can do is stand there.
>   sit there
>   lay there.
>   BE THERE.
>When language in any form would be a defilement? It feels in some way that you have died.
>Yet, you continue to live. Life itself is the most radical utterance you can summon. Then You have been initiated into the supernatural. There is a profound sense in which you now KNOW the depths of our mortal need for the LOVE of GOD.
>You really KNOW.
>Don't SPEAK!
>Touch the world with your Soul.
>Don't SPEAK!
>Let your heart embrace the wounded.
>Don't SPEAK!
>Share with God your hurtings.
>But, Don't SPEAK.
>Allow the Universe to open unto you.
>The Heavens to be pierced by your Humility.
>SPEAK NOT.
>The unvoiced ruminations of a Soul sequestered in PRAYER
>   will shape the NATIONS.
>   Bless the women.
>   Nurture the children
>   and teach Truth to humanity.
>GOD has been betrayed by words. And we need not depend on them when we Pray. Let us escape the seduction of WORDS when we kneel before GOD.

FOUR

We have used words to build walls; to deceive the innocent; to "distract" GOD; to avoid feeling; as a substitute for doing. Suddenly we are exposed to the power of WORDLESSNESS. The dignity of the UNSPOKEN. Consider Jesus before Herod:

> "He plied him with many questions,
> but Jesus gave him no answer."
>
> (Luke 23:9)

The barrage of words in the culture has rendered us
numb,
passive,
cynical,
pretentious,
carnal,
superficial,
unreflective and
spiritually lazy!

    There is a freedom that comes with the offering of SILENCE.
A depth of presence.
A power of discernment.
A sensate attunement.
RELEASE.
This is the time to be *shaped* by the SPIRIT.
This is the season of clarification and TRUTH.
Passion is cleansed and sanctified.
Righteousness emerges as a hallowed shining LIGHT.

FOUR

The rhythmn of Breath is a most beautiful part of SILENCE. In it, one can experience the mysterious flow of life. One comes to realize that we are indeed heavenly beings. By SILENCE, I am restored to perfection. I become ONE with all Beauty. Silence is the reservoir of the true aesthetic. I become ONE with Goodness. Silence is the tutor of every Virtue. By Silence, I am made whole. Because in Silence alone exists the unitive energies that call the Soul to GOD.

I cannot say it more emphatically! Let us love silence more than food, more than laughter, more than companionship. When I fast, I shall also keep silent. And in my JOY, I shall hide a sacred place for Silence. And though I journey with a thousand, I will heed the call of SILENCE to come apart and drink of my own authenticity.

Silence has many colors, odors and textures. The ARTIST, the PROPHET, and the TEACHER in me will discover her magic when once I surrender to her POWER. Silence can drape the Soul. Silence can intoxicate the heart. SILENCE, only Silence, can unravel the mysteries of GOD. This SILENCE is beautiful. Her fingers, like those of a skilled masseuse penetrate every area of resistance, tension and inflexibility. THIS SILENCE applauds the PRESENCE of love. This SILENCE heralds the dawn. THIS SILENCE is the echo of the footsteps of GOD.

I Follow them.
    STEP by STEP into the hidden regions of my Soul.
I Follow them.
    Along the Path of deep Revelation.
I Follow them.
    And enter the gates of TRUTH.

While in Namibia, the Spirit of the LORD came to me in SILENCE. In Silence have I learned the restorative power of Breath.

"Take the time to Breathe." The Spirit says.

"For in breathing you receive life.

In breathing you partake of the hidden mysteries of the Eternal. Take the time to breathe and know the wonder of your own mortality. Receive Every breath as a Kiss from GOD. Breath is LOVE. Let it flow!

Spend more TIME Breathing." My response has been to honor Silence 3 times a day—To CENTER. To FOCUS. To LISTEN. I enter the SILENCE. I REST in the ministry of my own Breathing Awareness. This is beautiful. This is Life. (I feel the difference in my Body! Amen.)

FOUR

In the morning, when I am awakened by the GREAT SILENCE, I will CENTER. To Center is to gather myself—mind, body and Soul. To Center is to present mySelf to the LORD as an offering. To Center is to allow the LOVE of GOD to become my Total Awareness. I will breathe in this SILENCE. By this Silence will I be Shaped. This is the Breath of NIA. (The Swahili word for PURPOSE.)

The KUJICHAGULIA Breath flows in the SILENCE at NOON or Mid day. In THIS Silence, I am taught to FOCUS. To quiet mySelf and be RESTORED to GOD's purpose for this Day. FOCUS. Breathe in Humility and GRACE. FOCUS. Wait with GOD. FOCUS. See the whole. To create, one must renounce the fear of SILENCE. Images shaped in Silence bring comfort, inspiration and TRUTH. Kujichagulia means self-determination. As I breathe, I am receiving POWER. This SILENCE is giving shape to my DESTINY. This SILENCE ignites a burning fire in my Soul. I am Still. Mine will be a surrendered breathing. A total neglect of action. I am STILL. I await the Breath of GOD.

This day will close with my vow to LISTEN. This is the BREATH of IMANI. Imani means Faith. No SILENCE is greater than this. The Cosmic hush when all creation concedes the GLORY of GOD. GOD, Eternally present. FOREVER Conscious. Totally Sensitive. The GOD who IS. This GOD IS AWAKE. And so I LISTEN. There are lessons from each day. On the meaning of the decisions I have made. Lessons. On the nature of my relationships. LESSONS. On the future of the world. LESSONS. On the manifestation of Beauty. I must LISTEN. I must be Taught. Let me in SILENCE now Breathe. I will LISTEN. By GOD's Spirit I shall be taught. And then the SILENCE will kiss me to sleep.

(NIA)
Morning

Dear GOD,
You Who inhabit
SILENCE;
Whose soundless Presence
infuses the world
with MYSTERY;

Awaken me
to the flow of Divinity
in my own Life.
　　　　Selah.

(KUJICHAGULIA)
Noon

Manifest the height and depth and breadth of my potentialities in the Universe.

FOUR

                      Amen

(IMANI)
Before Sleeping

Teach my Soul
to LOVE,
to Hear,
and to REST
in YOUR SILENCE.

                      Amen.

There are SEASONS in the Life of the Oblate when the "Call to SILENCE" is more   extensive,
           URGENT,
             profound,
             poetic or
             Healing.
When I hear the Call; I Obey.
When I sense the pull; I Respond.
If your world is over-worded or over-worked; Be SILENT and BREATHE.
Allow the SILENCE to make you whole.

The SILENCE of THE POOR

    For the Oblate, LOVE insists upon making your life an offering to the LORD. Unconditionally giving one' self <u>to</u> GOD is to at the same TIME give oneself <u>for</u> OTHERS.

    To penetrate the SILENCE of the poor is to open oneself at the deepest level to the groanings of the Universe for Epiphany.

    To become SILENT <u>with</u> the poor is to withstand the seduction of privatism, class interest and material idolatry.

    To WITNESS to the SILENCE of the POOR is to incarnate the Love of JESUS CHRIST.

    The SILENCE of the poor breeds <u>terror</u> in the hearts of the oppressive. They respond with weapons. The SILENCE of the poor stirs the soul of the ARTIST. The ARTIST responds with imagination. The SILENCE of the poor sows ambition in the hearts of the corrupt. The corrupt respond with self INTEREST. But in the Life of the Oblate,

FOUR

when her SILENCE is touched by the SILENCE of the poor; she responds with Solidarity.

So begins the Dance of Liberation.
Unseen.
Unspoken.
Unexpected.
UNDETERRED.
It is begun.

The gates of the Universe have been flung open by these Dancers of Judah. The women whose movements have been shaped by the GREAT SILENCE. Whose souls gyrate in anticipation of true deliverance. Unveiled we dance.
>Unashamed we dance.
>Fearless we dance.
>>Barefoot.
>>Bare headed.
>With nakedness of Soul.
>>WE DANCE.

To the rhythmn of an inner silence too penetrating to be ignored.

The one who does not fear her own SILENCE can never be defeated. For this reason, her Dance is a Dance of PRAISE. This is the Dance she will teach to her daughters. This Dance cannot be stolen, marketed or sabotaged. This Dance belongs to GOD.

The Silence of the POOR is the window of GOD. Through it GOD can see the integrity of the Church
> the courage of the Oblate
> and the heart of the Nations.

From their side, the POOR are also looking. Through the *opening* window of their SILENCE they can trace the footsteps of Eternity;
watch the sun setting on the reign of the wicked; call out to the Visionaries, Martyrs and artists that have gone before them and
Welcome the Herald of justice, Righteousness and the HEALING of the NATIONS.

The courageous PRAY TO KNOW SILENCE and to Love her.

From my window in Johannesburg, I pray to the LORD, Listening to the SILENCE that covers me. Tasting the Silence that fills my mouth.

DANCE OF THE UNSPOKEN • 117

FOUR

Waiting.
Listening and WAITING.
Open.
Open to the SILENCE of GOD.
Repentant.
Resilient.
Renewed.

    All the way from the Kingdom of Swaziland, the SILENCE followed me.
Spoke to me from the beautiful mountains.
        in the eyes of the school children.
          on the tables laden with mangos, bananas and
            pineapples.
  I listened.
  I know.
  I wait.
  I am not afraid anymore!
This Silence is a Sacred Gift.
By it shall the NATIONS be Healed.

    What is that sound that disturbs the sleep of the evil ones? Haunts the comfortable? Provokes the unbeliever? It is the sound of SILENCE. The Silence of the poor.

      "Let anyone who has an ear
      Listen to what the Spirit
      is saying to the churches." (Rev. 2:17)

Dear Cojourner,
    PRAY to
        LISTEN and
            TO OBEY.

      "Silently now I wait for Thee
      Ready my God, Thy will to see . . .
      Open my heart, illumine me.
      Saviour divine."
            (A.M.E. Hymnal #285)

FOUR

By the POWER of SILENCE, I am being taught to live "inside-out." What I believe, feel, know and HOPE. That which I pray and long for. The Visions that sustain me. The music that bathes me. All these must be re-deposited in the Universe. The Christ of Faith is a cosmic Deity. The space of the TRIUNE is without borders of knowledge, experience or manifestation. This is the GOD, who to know is not to know.

Who to encounter is to be totally Amazed! And to receive GOD's anointing is neither to "possess" it or govern it!

Thus inside-out living is to attempt to have my reality shaped by Christ in me! To do so is to be authentic. To do so is to order my world with an adventuresome integrity. To know Truth, I go within. LISTEN. Obey.

It is here that I first learned the POWER and imperative of
Self-emptying.
de-junking.
the death of habit by means of starvation!

My inner world was "congested" with roles, false images of myself, an over consumption of "appropriates," spiritual misdemeanors, emotional holocausts, racial anxiety, intergenerational fears, incomplete theologies, unhealthy relationships, cultural paranoia, mood swings, terror of the first magnitude, RAGE, affection deprivation and miscellaneous indulgences.

Whew!

I can Breathe again.

Got to get it all out Cojourner. Got to get it ALL OUT. All of it! Only then can the authentic Soul prevail. And all the Beauty—unmarred;

all the Truth—unperjured;

all the LOVE—uncorrupted;

by the POWER of the Holy Spirit will flow from the "inside" out.

You can never truly discover ALL that GOD has deposited in you for the UNIVERSE—

You can never fully perceive ALL that the UNIVERSE holds for you—

You will never flow in authentic Divinity—until you are taught by the Spirit the reality of "INSIDE-OUT" Living.

Selah.

"Hannah was praying in her heart, and her lips were moving but her voice was not heard . . ."
(I Samuel 1:13)

FOUR

Wordless utterances issue from "a woman deeply troubled" (I Samuel 1:15) Wordless desire pours from the Soul of a woman whose eyes have grown dim watching for the coming of the LORD. Wordless Praise issues from the exhausted frame of the woman who makes the hazardous trek from the eastern shore of Maryland to an unknown Canadian freedom. Could Harriet Tubman have remained in slavery once the SPIRIT OF GOD "constrained" her to pursue the impossible? What word is there to "explain" the Call. One can only give one's body in assent. Our bodies hear and understand the Silence of GOD. And yes, our bodies do say a WORD to the LORD. Perhaps not in the audible vernacular of the "religious" or the wise. Nevertheless, the limp arms raised to greet the death angel, really do SPEAK. The torrent of undulation that reverberates from the perspiration soaked, shoeless body before the altar SPEAKS. There is language in the body "slain" by the POWER of the overshadowing. The moment I invite Jesus Christ to become LORD of my life, I "receive" the Holy Ghost. I, therefore, become a vessel of inhabitation! And "deep calls to deep." Spirit to Spirit. Life to Life. Light to Light. There is a "treasure in this earthen vessel." (2 COR. 4:7)

This is the "abiding." The "Living in." **Inhabitation** of the first magnitude. The Spirit of the LORD *in me* communing and communicating both with me and with TRINITY, our God. For this reason, let the life of the Oblate be "self controlled, upright, holy and disciplined." (Titus 1:8)

"because if you confess with your lips that Jesus is Lord and believe in your heart that God raised him from the dead, you will be saved."
(Romans 10:9)

"Jesus said to them again, "Peace be with you. As the Father has sent me, so I send you." When he had said this, he breathed on them and said to them, "Receive the Holy Spirit."
(John 20:22)

FOUR

"Now therefore, if you obey my voice and keep my covenant, you shall be my treasured possession out of all the peoples. Indeed, the whole earth is mine,"

(Exodus 19:5)

Dear CoJourner, I engage a profound contradiction, as I attempt to "speak" of the thing which has no words. There is a "knowing," a Reality, a spiritual intelligence of depths too sublime to be articulated! Authentic pain has no word. Authentic Joy has no word. Both have tears! Both have a body response that emits a weakening like sensation. Yet they are opposites. WORD is incomplete. We need a body! When God told Israel, "You will be my people, and I will be your GOD;" God could not fully communicate this message until GOD demonstrated the same in the *body* of Jesus Christ. To LOVE the LORD, my word is insufficient, I need a body!

This is why the meaning of **Inhabitation** is so incredible *and* so critical to the Faith of the Oblate. There must be a welcoming of the Spirit of the LORD. There must be an **Inhabitation** "consciousness"— the "knowing."

"Christ *in* me, the HOPE of GLORY."
(Col. 1:27)

"IN" me. Too incomprehensible to explain.
IN me. Too apocalyptic to decipher.
IN me. More wondrous and expansive than the Universe itself. One needs time to contemplate this unto revelation. Such that God makes it known as reality!
IN me.
The Living GOD of the Universe is LIVING in ME.
IN me.
Every Divine Virtue, Grace and intention is LIVING IN ME.
IN me.
The whole Self-understanding of the TRINITY and all manner of Supernatural meaning is LIVING in ME.
IN me. THE CREATOR.
IN me. THE MESSIAH.
IN me. THE CONSOLATION OF THE WORLD.

Selah

THE VESSEL of INHABITATION

FOUR

"For thus says the high and lofty one who **inhabits** eternity, whose name is Holy: I dwell in the high and holy place, and also with those who are contrite and humble in spirit, to revive the spirit of the humble, and to revive the heart of the contrite."

(Isaiah 57:15)

It is at once a happy and troubling occasion to acknowledge mySelf to be the Living Space of God. Happy because of the unrequited need for inclusion. Troubling because of the awesome sense of unworthiness, Happy, because I don't have to explain it. Troubling because I CAN'T explain it! Both Happy and Troubling because I and everyone else can see it and neither I nor anyone can stop it!

This is a MATTER of the Soul.

Incredible as it actually IS; the Soul agonizes over the controversies of Inhabitation with "groanings too deep for the mind to language." I fear going "off the deep end." It seemed such a simple issue at first. *And now, here I am in a large and vacuous place. There is neither night or day. Burnished sands extend from the heavenlies covered by a deep aqua and sometimes midnight blue density. When I close my eyes, there is nothing there. I see nothing there. Until I open my heart. And then I see trees laughing in graceful promenade. Thunder shakes the moon from her place and a thousand sparrows flee from the sight there of. God is crying. God is crying.*

"Why do we fast, but you do not see? Why humble ourselves, but you do not notice? Look, you serve your own interest on your fast day, and oppress all your workers. Look, you fast only to quarrel and to fight and to strike with a wicked fist. Such fasting as you do today will not make your voice heard on high."

(Isaiah 58:3,4)

"Likewise the Spirit helps us in our weakness; for we do not know how to pray as we ought, but that very Spirit intercedes with sighs too deep for words."

(Romans 8:26)

FOUR

"... for I carry the marks of Jesus branded on my body."

(Galatians 6:17b)

I wish it were midnight. When I can see the heavenlies without distraction. I wish it were midnight when the whole world is a meadow (except for TIMES SQUARE)! I wish it were midnight when sky turbulence ceases over the ocean of my disappointment. The notion of God in tears mirrors and magnifies 1,000 fold my own sense of vulnerability. My Soul is stretched and "I bear in my body the marks of Jesus Christ."
The RISK of **Inhabitation** is a Soul Life independent of will, ambition, and appetite. An interior Coup détat. Reason is defeated. Yet a Superior intelligence—WISDOM—ascends.
We are Wisdom's daughters who follow the Son and do not betray our vows.
We are Wisdom's daughters who do not fear the Silence of LOVE.
We are Wisdom's daughters who embrace the nations with our prayers.
Our veils have been removed.
Yokes broken.
Bodies healed.
We teach our children the beauty of Silence. To honor her ways. To celebrate her gifts.
In SILENCE we pour strength into the hearts of our men. Our souls in Silence unite with the courage of every woman in all generations.
THIS SILENT FIRE is rising throughout the Universe.

Selah.

This, for me, is the most powerful and intimidating experience. The unWORDing of Passion. Having been birthed in a verbal religious culture. And by personality and gift being inclined to that which is spoken. I am now standing over against myself. The end thereof is the cultivation of the Life of the Soul. At times I want to cry out, to justify, to mourn, to exhilarate, to capture the moment with a song.
For now, I will submit to my Body as my Voice.
"How can these things be?" (Luke 1:34)
Who can know?
I begin by trusting my body to know herSelf, to discover herSelf, to honor herSelf. To LOVE herSelf.
I will silence the inner critic of my Body.
I will woo the Gift with benedictions of Grace.
I will say of my Body:
> "You belong to me.
> You have been given LIFE by the
> > LORD, God.
> You are the channel of the
> > Holy Ghost.
> I accept and honor your Beauty.
> With you I shall make
> "acceptable" prayers unto the
> > LORD.
> In you I shall penetrate the
> walls of the Mystery
> > of SILENCE.
> In the Name of
> JESUS. Amen."

FOUR

"Praise is due to you, O God, in Zion; and to you shall vows be performed, O you who answer prayer! To you all flesh shall come."

(Psalms 65:2)

FOUR

"Then Ezra blessed the LORD, the great God, and all the people answered, "Amen, Amen," lifting up their hands. Then they bowed their heads and worshipped the LORD with their faces to the ground."

(Nehemiah 8:6)

It is the ministry of SILENCE to illumine, to echo, to heal and to restore.

Some of the movements of my Body are clearly vowels. Strong. Definitive. Giving Shape to new meanings. Many are consonants. Joining powers to communicate a message. Cohesion is neither necessary or unnecessary. I am seeking to live for God *in* my Body! There are so many moments of pause, hesitation, interlude. It's a matter of being born anew. A *liberating* discomfort. To live an unmodulated presence on the planet.

Having wrestled with Silence all this time; there is a roaring lion within me. An ocean with no boundaries. A bright and shining light. I long for God. To whom I would speak with my own VOICE. My own Word. My own Song. *In* my Body. *In* my very own Body.

The sins *against* our bodies have intimidated woman. Ashamed to know our own feelings. To express our own rhythms. To move in a personal sense of poetry. To flow with full imagination. Until at last we die. And we are buried *in* our bodies. For even in death there are few who hope to escape them. This is what incest, mockery, rape, cultural sabotage, residual Puritanism, pornography, sexism, racism and incomplete theologies have done to us! A relentless body heritage of shame. Unbearable shame. SHAME. Shame. Shame. Nevertheless. I *believe*. There is being released in *this* body the POWER to heal the nations. An interior summit of divine potentialities—LOVE, HOPE, REDEMPTION and GENEROSITY—convened by my indomitable Soul.

**Search your heart for ways
to bless your BODY.
PRAY the LOVE of
    GOD to Heal you
    of every residue of SHAME.
WRITE an Affirmation that
    Celebrates *YOUR* BODY:**

I am host to the Tabernacling of the Past and the Future. What a treasure the body is. Listen to the bodies of the women in the PIETA of John Biggers and the paintings of Kathleen Atkins Wilson. The voices of our bodies language the Vision of Life with candor, passion, meaning. Unrehearsed, our bodies speak. Call out. Worship. Invoke. Inquire. Even when we find ourselves entrenched in a wordless experience. Consequently when my body is endued with the POWER and PRESENCE of the Holy Spirit; *in* my Body I can speak Holiness. The scriptures indicate that the very *shadows* of the Apostles brought healing!

This sanctified body is a MIRACLE in the transition—from "perishable to imperishable." The "treasure" in the Vessel is the source of the GLORY.

    Chaos approaches; but cannot enter. I will not be "entangled again with the yokes of bondage: (2 Peter 2:20) delusions of control of myself or
    others.
    "artificial" needs.
    not even the "rewards" of ambition. I too have been shown "the Kingdoms of this world." I remain untempted ONLY because I have been LOVED. LOVE has brought my life to perfection.

My body can RElease
    fear and tension.
My body can REceive
    affection and tenderness.
My body gives herSelf to the REfreshing.
    This is Life.
    This is fullness.
    This is GOD's will for me, for us,
        for the nations!

What language is there for such a reality? Whose vocabulary can rightly express such an experience? Is there a lexicon that aptly discerns the Supernatural? What after all is a miracle, if it's GOD you are asking?

    Can it be called by any name other than LOVE? This is the one thing that the blind *can* see and the deaf *can* hear. LOVE. It is language that the body can speak, if only it remains free of the deceptions of the mind!

FOUR

"So it is with the resurrection of the dead. What is sown is perishable, what is raised is imperishable. It is sown in dishonor, it is raised in glory. It is sown in weakness, it is raised in power. It is sown a physical body, it is raised a spiritual body. If there is a physical body, there is also a spiritual body."

(1 Corinthians 15:42–44)

"Again, the devil took him to a very high mountain and showed him all the kingdoms of the world and their splendor; and he said to him, "All these I will give you, if you will fall down and worship me."

(Matthew 4:8,9)

FOUR

How incredibly angry we have been with our bodies. How we have consented to a stunted and vilifying eroticism. How we must repossess our bodies in complete wordless affirmation. Allowing the Holy Spirit to minister new memories and healing expectations to every dimension of ourselves.

As you become the vessel of renewal; share in this BODY Meditation. In your Spirit, hear the words of JESUS. "COME UNTO ME." THE UNSPOKEN CALL on the next page is a special opportunity to consciously surrender your body in prayer. As you internalize the following thought, you will become wonderfully receptive to the gift of BODY Meditation:

I know that I shall consent to allow every cell in my body to hear this invitation to blessing. Otherwise, I shall be/remain tense.
    cramped.
    rigid.
    anxious.
    diseased.

My full body longs to HEAR
these words, "COME UNTO ME."
RESPOND to these words, "COME UNTO ME."
EMBRACE the Spirit of the LORD in these words.
    "COME UNTO ME."

I open mySelf to the
SPIRIT of THE LORD.

Cousel To my CoJourner:
    In preparation, read through to Selah. Then close this book for a time and give your body to the Unspoken. Once again, take several deep breaths to quiet yourself and *PRAY* to fully *enter* the meditation. It may be helpful to visualize the Cross or the letters that spell the name of JESUS.
    (Spend 7–20 minutes)
Conclude with the LORD'S PRAYER.

THE UNSPOKEN CALL

"Come Unto Me" (Matthew 11:28)
"Come Unto Me" (Matthew 14:29)
"Come Unto Me"
Heard from a distance.
Heard in the midst of fatigue, turmoil and infirmity.
Heard deep in the wilderness of my suffering.
Heard when all my tears have been wasted and my soul is parched and aching.
Heard when midnight passes into morning.

Heard because ecstasy has exhausted herself and become quiet.
Heard in the moment of VICTORY.
Heard at the point of my failure.
Heard as Silence within Silence.

My body now rests.
    lets go.
    unwinds.
    sinks into GOD's presence.
There is no word for this season.
My body is my Voice.
      Selah.

FOUR

"The Spirit and the bride say, "Come." And let everyone who hears say, "Come." And let everyone who is thirsty come. Let anyone who wishes take the water of life as a gift."

(Revelation 22:17)

"Then the priests and the Levites stood up and blessed the people, and their voice was heard; their prayer came to his holy dwelling in heaven."

(2 Chronicles 30:27)

FOUR

It is a radical consideration for some that PRAYER can be WORDless. Surely it is a matter of the Heart! As I seek to make my life a love offering unto the LORD—an Oblation. My thoughts, my feelings, my very will honor the FLOW of the SPIRIT of God *in* me!

Body PRAYER is *not* performance. It is unto the LORD. Yet, it can be Healing, Energizing, calming or Refreshing. Body PRAYER can be Solitary or Corporate. But NEVER choreographed. The SPIRITUAL DIRECTOR serves to guide, to discern, to intercede but not to choreograph! PRAYER is a Spiritual issue. It is a matter of the heart.

There are as many dimensions of PRAYER as there are experiences with GOD. As a "help" to those who wish to experience the Reality of Body PRAYER. To explore the depths of their own unspokenness. Please receive this offering.

SOUL DANCE

SISTER'S EVE, the Night Before the NIGHT BEFORE CHRISTMAS, when the Souls of women gather to celebrate our "Mary-ness."
Bodies pocketed for miracles.
Pour libations in memory of women whose pain goes unnoticed.
Hold hands in circles to embrace the Hope of the world.
Light a Candle.
And wait.
For the Cosmic labor to begin.
Go Home in Silence.
To wait.
For the Delivery.
    the Proclamation.
    and the coming of the Wise men.

Living Soulfully is an incarnating experience. A Body "overshadowed" by and "filled" with the Holy Spirit is an oceanic reality. There is movement that emanates from the very depths of LOVE through the pores of the flesh of the Cojourner. SOUL DANCE is one third LONGING, one third HOPE and one third IMAGINATION. TRUE PRAYER. PRAYER in which the Cojourner is completely given to GOD. This praying is exhausting, energizing and liberating. Such praying Heals. As in every Dance, there are *TRANSITION* movements. This is sacred time.

DANCE OF THE UNSPOKEN

The Dancer draws in her energy,
    quiets her body.
    listens to the Holy Spirit
    and inwarldy prepares for
    the next step.

FOUR

SOUL DANCE is personal.
SOUL DANCE is Spirit Talk.
SOUL DANCE is honest.
SOUL DANCE is the un-worded language of Holy LOVE.
SOUL DANCE is unto the LORD.
SOUL DANCE is child-like.
SOUL DANCE is wisdom.

I now begin to give my Body to PRAYER. To actively, actually commune with GOD *in* my Body. Allowing myself a season of silent meditation on GOD's LOVE for me; I yield to the Holy Spirit and PRAY to the LORD with "ALL my heart, my soul, my mind, my strength *and* MY BODY." I stay in each dimension until I am RELEASED to the next! I remember that PRAYER is LOVE. And I am NOT ashamed. PRAYER IS LOVE.

(Dear CoJourner, silently pray the LORD's prayer at any *time* to bring closure.)

Flow with me or away from me for that matter into the 12 dimensions of wordless PRAYER—Soul Dance. The first is *INVOCATION*. I am inviting the Spirit. Wooing the Presence. Calling the Power. Visualize Icons of Mary in labor in Bethlehem. Become one with her in adoration and hope, longing and grief. Draw deep into any personal history of births and rebirths. In your Body Reach for God. Be born in God. Be gloriously translated to a heightened consciousness of GOD. WELCOME the SPIRIT of the LORD with your body.
                        in your body.
        Reach for GOD.
        Using your Body as your Voice
        Call OUT to the LOVE of GOD.

INVOCATION

                TRANSITION
Center and Prepare yourself in MIND, BODY and ENERGY to CHANGE DIRECTION, PACE AND MOVEMENT.

FOUR   **AWAKENING**   Then comes the *AWAKENING*. (the 2nd dimension). The POWER of GOD shakes the Universe and my DESTINY is awakened. My sense of Purpose is awakened. My "sleeping" gifts are awakened. With my Body, I begin to PRAY—

    "WISDOM of GOD, AWAKEN in ME.
    Creativity of GOD, AWAKEN in ME.
    LAUGHTER of Heaven, AWAKEN in ME.
    Come playful Spirit come.
    Come thankful Spirit come.
    Come compassionate Spirit come.
    Come Messiah, Come.!"

I experience every cell in my body ignited with the Name of JESUS. Every cell. Every cell. Every system in my body is infused with the Knowledge of His Resurrection:

Cardiovascular
respiratory
digestive
nervous
Indocrine
Skeletal
Muscular
Circulatory

Every faculty and function and organ in my body begin to resonate with the memory of the baptism of JESUS.

Hallelujah.

Each of my senses:
    sight
    taste
    touch
    smell
    hearing

are indued with the POWER of Refreshing that JESUS experienced at the edge of the wilderness when Angels came and ministered to him. (Matthew 4:11)

TRANSITION
Center and Prepare yourself in MIND, BODY and ENERGY to CHANGE DIRECTION, PACE AND MOVEMENT.

FOUR

Immediately, I am grace readied for the 3rd dimension. *REPENTANCE.* I throw myself at the foot of the cross. I prostrate myself. I hide my face. I bow down. I crawl on my knees. I bow down. I humiliate mySelf. I bow down. My body screams "LORD have mercy upon me, a sinner." I bow down.

REPENTANCE

    The rigidities of guilt and shame vanish.
    I leap out of the grip of UNFORGIVENESS.
    I acknowledge *my* sins.
    I take responsibility for my failures.
    I call on the Holy Spirit to re-shape my Response to others.
I cast before the LORD all the tokens of my disobedience. All the trinkets of my willful indulgence. I lay in the ashes of Pardon.

FOUR

OFFERING

"But the king said to Araunah, "No, but I will buy them from you for a price; I will not offer burnt offerings to the LORD my God that cost me nothing." So David bought the threshing floor and the oxen for fifty shekels of silver."

(2 Samuel 24:24)

WAIT

RELEASE

"Cast your burden on the LORD, and he will sustain you; he will never permit the righteous to be moved."

(Psalms 55:22)

TRANSITION
Center and Prepare yourself in MIND, BODY and ENERGY to CHANGE DIRECTION, PACE AND MOVEMENT.

I kneel at the gate of the Fourth Dimension.

Only now can I offer mySelf. Purged. Cleansed. Forgiven. FORGIVING. I make a LOVE *Offering* of my Life to the LORD. I offer back to Him my capacity to HOPE.

To Him I offer the dreams and VISIONS of Revelation. To God I make an offering of ALL my body memories. The Gate opens. This "living sacrifice" (Romans 12:1) is accepted. All praises to God's Holy Name.

TRANSITION
Center and Prepare yourself in MIND, BODY and ENERGY to CHANGE DIRECTION, PACE AND MOVEMENT.

In exchange for my offering, I am offered the fifth Dimension—the privilege of *WAITING*! And so I **WAIT**. Through the protests of ego, I **WAIT**. In the discomfort of unanswered prayer, I **WAIT**. While the jubilee of the ungodly encompasses the earth, I **WAIT**. As the congregations empty the sanctuaries bereft of Vision, I **WAIT**. Until humility like a tender sapling is planted in my Soul, I **WAIT**. Until. . . . .

TRANSITION
Center and Prepare yourself in MIND, BODY and ENERGY to CHANGE DIRECTION, PACE AND MOVEMENT.

Re-lease-ing, the 6th Dimension of Silence is awkward initially. I had not realized how much I was holding on to and why. The latter issue being the most frightening and disdainful.

Can I trust God without my parachute!?
Can I let go of the dull pain?
the boring familiar?
the anticipated rejection?
the pre-meditated ostracism?
the impotent grace?
the unkind traditions?

the ungodly attitudes and relationships?
the destructive dependencies?
the pride?
I Can.
Yes, I Can.
I let go!
I LET it all GO.
I *Release* everything that has kept me bound.
I RELEASE UNTO the LORD.

FOUR

TRANSITION
Center and Prepare yourself in MIND, BODY and ENERGY to CHANGE DIRECTION, PACE AND MOVEMENT.

Release flows unobstructed into *YIELDING*, the 7th Dimension. Surrendering to God. Total and complete non-resistance. The Collapse of volition in the arms of infinity. It is as though the plug has been pulled out of the sky and the entire life force begins to pour steadily into my Soul. Amen.

YIELDING

    I open my desire to the flow of Divine LOVE
        in the Universe
    My Soul pursues the LIVING GOD.
    My thoughts
    My heart
    My hands and
    My feet are carried by the Wind of Holy desire.
    I am weightless.
        burdenless.
        fearless.
        needless.
    There is only GOD, mySelf and this moment. FOREVER.

FOUR

TRANSITION
Center and Prepare yourself in MIND, BODY and ENERGY to CHANGE DIRECTION, PACE AND MOVEMENT.

EMBRACE   The 8th Dimension of Silence takes place when the Believer *"embraces"* the VISION of God. Nothing Less. Without controversy or reluctance. The Cosmic "YES" is uttered from within.

My Soul leaps and whirls in ecstasy as I discover the magnitude of the Supernatural within my reach and beyond my Grasp. My imagination enters regions of undiscovered creativity. I am ALIVE. I open my LIFE to receive   All Creation.
>All Nature.
>All humanity.
>All children.
>All rhythms.
>All music.
>All possibility.

LOVE emanates from my very shadow. The mantle of prophecy tossed from heaven lights upon my shoulders and I wear it well!

TRANSITION
Center and Prepare yourself in MIND, BODY and ENERGY to CHANGE DIRECTION, PACE AND MOVEMENT.

FORMATION   The work of the Holy Spirit is actively manifested in the 9th Dimension. This is the season of *formation*. One's Soul life is shaped by Divine Purpose.

"God said to Moses, "I AM WHO I AM." He said further, "Thus you shall say to the Israelites, 'I AM has sent me to you."

(Exodus 3:14)

I am stretched out in the imagination of GOD.
I am purged of delusion.
I am filled with the manna of the Kingdom.
I am clothed in Purple raiment.
In the mirror of my Soul;
>I see the LIGHT of God Reflected.

In the eyes of Eternity I behold REST and assurance.
I have become who I AM.
The Supernatural "I AM" echoes deep within me.
I am the image of "I AM."

DANCE OF THE UNSPOKEN • 135

" . . . and he is named
    Wonderful Counselor,
    Mighty God,
    Everlasting Father,
    Prince of Peace."
              (Isaiah 9:6)

FOUR

My identify and my Reality are ONE.

TRANSITION
Center and Prepare yourself in MIND, BODY and ENERGY to CHANGE DIRECTION, PACE AND MOVEMENT.

RESPONDING makes the 10th Dimension an exhilarating season of Silence. The illumined Path is my reality. I am seized by it. It is clear, definite, beautiful, MINE. My Soul quakes. My heart roars. My Body becomes a field of irruptions. The Kingdom belongs to me.

RESPONDING

Touched; I touch.
Blessed; I bless.
Loved; I love.
Heard; I listen.
Called; I invoke.
Released; I dance!
There are not enough colors to express me.
        enough moons to enchant me.
        enough rivers to baptize me.
        enough languages to communicate ME.
Now that I cannot die!

TRANSITION
Center and Prepare yourself in MIND, BODY and ENERGY to CHANGE DIRECTION, PACE AND MOVEMENT.

What can follow this, but *REST*. I must quiet my Spirit in the LOVE of God. For in this life, my witness must be "in the body." I cannot leave mySelf behind. The 11th Dimension will result from discipline of Soul. For the Spirit is too much for the Body. Amen. **So the 11th dimension may be exercised at any time.**

REST

"Therefore my heart is glad, and my soul rejoices; my body also rests secure."

              (Psalms 16:9)

FOUR

TRANSITION
Center and Prepare yourself in MIND, BODY and ENERGY to CHANGE DIRECTION, PACE AND MOVEMENT.

RETURN

RETURN. This is the 12th Dimension of Silence. At-one-ment. I center mySelf in the universe of my vocation. I belong. My Soul is at home in my body.

At the end of a journey, a song, a book, a prayer.
At whatever moment there is an ending—
a relationship
a meal
a gathering
there must be a ceremony of RETURN—not to former things; for life is ever flowing, changing!
At every ending; let there be a ceremony of return to the confession of Faith,
    covenant of Purpose,
    devotion to Life,
    submission to JESUS.

In RETURN, I experience balance, wonder, serenity and freedom. My body is more Alive. My mind also. And oh the ecstasy of my Soul!

SILENTLY PRAY THE LORD'S PRAYER at any time to bring closure to your season of PRAYER.

"GLORY be to the Father,
and to the Son,
and to the Holy Ghost.
As it was in the beginning,
is now,
and ever shall be.
World without end.
Amen."

FOUR

Dear Cojourner,

Every TRANSITION has brought me closer and closer to my own Quiet Center. Every TRANSITION has strengthened my resolve to pursue the vision. Soul Dance teaches me the POWER of the UNSPOKEN. Does your BODY now have a "word" for

    INVOCATION

    AWAKENING

    REPENTANCE?

What are the inner directives that shape

    OFFERING

    WAIT

    RELEASE?

Having made full benefit of your TRANSITIONS, what is your BODY VOICE for

    YIELDING

    EMBRACE

    FORMATION?

With your new "door of utterance" have you explored a fresh vocabulary for

    RESPONDING

    REST

    RETURN?

SOUL DANCE means refusing to "store up" hurt, idea, mood or image. It means giving expression to the full range of meanings in my Christian journey. SOUL DANCE means having a way to GOD that is from the heart and through the body.

SOUL DANCE entitles me to shake and shape the meaning of life's heaviness, PRAYER has become more spontaneous.

More OPEN.

    SIMPLE.

    HONEST.

With such ease in Praying, Hearing GOD.

        SEEING GOD.

            TOUCHING GOD. Has become more profound and entirely contagious!

FOUR

The heart of a genuine Oblate can fill a Cathedral with the Spirit of Prayer. One pure and unblemished PROSTRATION will send rivers of healing through the universe. Apocalyptic struggle and wonder surround the Oblate. Intense rejection or/and intense solidarity mark the response of those experiencing the Apostolate for the first time. SOUL DANCE is her one opportunity to be endued with GODsight as she embraces Destiny. After all, One prays to SEE. Dances to See! Waits, just to SEE!

This is a time of subtle terror. A time when the Dancer is most vulnerable to the distractions of feeling and circumstance. Obey LOVE. Listen to the SPIRIT of GOD. TRANSITIONS are the most beautiful and magical seasons of our lives. Unpredictable and fertile. The vast potentialities of Soul life can be released or trapped. Do not become psychologically captive to your TRANSITION. If you do, you will never move on to the Ultimate Purpose, which is sight. The gateway to WISDOM. REVELATION comes to the Dancer as Vision. REVELATION comes through the Dancer as an oracle of GOD. Soul Dance is a fundamentally *inward* move of the seeker. When the paths of knowing are set before you; choose SILENCE. As the living space of God, your invocation will be chaste. Choose Silence that your AWAKENING will be complete and your REPENTANCE uncompromised. Only in SILENCE can the OFFERING of the Oblate remain undefiled and her WAITING be transformed into a sacrament. TO RELEASE, to YIELD and to EMBRACE are the three MOVEMENTS in SILENCE that bring the DANCER greater dimensions of open-ness. To have chosen the PATH of SILENCE is the genesis of Oblate interior FORMATION. This sacramental SILENCE breathes integrity in our RESPONDING, faith in the one called to REST and the Courage to RETURN to the light of the VISION.

What poverty for the believer who has not escaped the snares of "exterior" religion. Whose heart has not become the voice of her prayer Life. What dullness of Spirit for she whose thought realm is not endued with the authentic PRESENCE of the LIGHT. I have grown weary of much or often speaking to mySelf of GOD. *SILENCE* is teaching me to allow the SPIRIT of the LORD to communicate with me God's own thoughts.

The Journey inward prepares the way for and sustains the blessing of **Inhabitation**. This is the genesis of perpetual prayer.

The audible, the exterior, fade. The inward, the unspoken, **REIGN**. The body is the Holy SPACE of the SPIRIT of God. This is an experiential Spirituality. Our LORD has said humanity would no longer need to be taught GOD. (Jeremiah 31:34) All the issues of human culture are reconciled in the Dance of the Unspoken. "Come and See." You too will discover where Jesus Lives! That the Kingdom of GOD is within you! (Luke 17:21)

FOUR

"As for you, the anointing that you received from him abides in you, and so you do not need anyone to teach you. But as his anointing teaches you about all things, and is true and is not a lie, and just as it has taught you, abide in him."

(1 John 2:27)

FOUR

SHEER BRILLIANCE—
DESIGNED FOR THE UNSPOKEN

"But the king will rejoice in God; all who swear by God's name will praise him, while the mouths of liars will be silenced. (Psalm 63:11)

As I learn to hear my body. As I bridge the distance between my acknowledged spirituality and my body. It is liberating to begin to understand that my body *also* has a desire for GOD. And great consolation is aroused by the discovery that "the streams of God are filled with water." (Psalm 65:9) Surely, in our fatigue, infirmity, discouragement and emptiness, it is our desire to enter "the streams of God." Surely, this is the whole dignity of PRAYER. Surely, the Oblate can have no surer benediction under heaven! So often my body is a remarkable living parable of my spiritual condition: Stimulated. relaxed. Anxious.

    dehydration.
    anemia.
    obesity.
    insomnia—
    malnutrition.
    fatigue.
    longing.

TO THE CoJourner:
Yes, there is a need for God in my body. There is a way by which PRAYER can make itself known *in* the body. Total PRAYER is leaping off the diving board of invocation into the Oceanic LOVE of God. Language is useless. Vocabulary avails nothing. Prayer is absolute when I give my body to the LORD in PRAYER. The only "helps" available for what is now being offered is to remember to say in your heart:

> **"I am as beautiful in the eyes of God as an infant struggling to walk for the first time."**
> **"This is my body, the living space of GOD."**
> **"I am designed for the Unspoken."**

Let these affirmations encourage you to risk into the realm of blessing. Hear the song of Creation as your body communes with GOD for you. May your heart be uplifted. Your mind and memory also. Don't take "NO" for an answer or "fear" as a crutch! You are designed for PRAYER. There is an inner LIGHT that will burst into the heavens when you are fully endued! Make this your diamond Oblation. SHINE with GOD's glory. You CAN do this. Salvation is worth it.

FOUR

Beloved Cojourner, prepare to be amazed!

Silence the inner-critic and take the plunge. Give yourSelf to the Lord for **90 minutes of RADIANCE INTENT**.
Page 143 provides guidelines for unlocking the splender.
Pages 144 to 159 represent 13 unique opportunities to pray, to listen, to Journal and to be transformed. Devote 90 minutes to each.
You deserve it! Just remember that 90 minutes in *not* long in terms of Eternity. It is only a beginning. Be attentive to the Holy SPIRIT. Listen to your body. Relax. Be Loved. Breathe. Remain undistracted. You *can* do THIS. You are worth it!

    Let the GLORY reign! Let your heart exult and be glad! Let the Silence of God be released like a flood. Let every cell in your body tingle with **Inhabitation**! Let your body know itself as Beloved. As Sanctuary. As host. Your beginnings may *feel* clumsy. Awkward. Uncoordinated. Heavy. Unsophisticated. However uncomfortable your beginnings—**BEGIN**!

FOUR

For those of us who wish to make a cohesive beginning; yet feel intimidated by the time frame. The following suggestion may prove helpful:

Silence	2 minutes
Transition	3 minutes
Praying The Text	7 minutes
Prostration	3 minutes
Listen	3 minutes
Soul Dance	8 minutes
Transition	3 minutes
Silence	3 minutes
Praying The Text	7 minutes
Prostration	3 minutes
Silence	3 minutes
Transition	3 minutes
Soul Dance	8 minutes
Listen	3 minutes
Journalling	12 minutes
Silence	3 minutes
Transition	3 minutes
Soul Dance	7 minutes
Silence	3 minutes
THE LORD'S PRAYER	3–5 minutes

FOUR

However incomprehensible our beginnings; however "self" conscious. I know the end thereof will be Health and Refreshing. Reflect on these thoughts: "My Body desires this moment. My mind is the soil of Eternity awaiting the seeds that will be sown by His SPIRIT. My Soul and my emotion have opened unto the language of GRACE. My lips are sealed! I don't have to speak.
My heart shall learn to Hear GOD in the SCRIPTURES, to pursue the LORD IN PRAYER and to yield to the movement of the HOLY SPIRIT."

UNLOCKING THE SPLENDER

It is one of the un-named benefits of PRAYER and Meditation that by the power of SOUL I am able to Re imagine mySelf in the universe. Optional Helps:

1) Invite the SPIRIT of the LORD to come to you in the text.

2) Experience your body "hearing" the scripture.

3) Awaken your deepest thought realm to the Meditation.

4) Be Silent.

5) Start Over.

6) Be Silent.

7) "WRITE down the Revelation and MAKE it Plain." (Habakkuk 2:2)

It is NOT imperative to pursue the devotions in sequence. Make a beginning then proceed to page 158. Return to this section from TIME TO TIME as the SPIRIT leads.

FOUR

"Therefore, my friends, since we have confidence to enter the sanctuary by the blood of Jesus, by the new and living way that he opened for us through the curtain (that is, through his flesh),"

(Hebrews 10:19,20)

As I begin to consider the Gift of the Body of Jesus Christ, I become mute. The fact that this crucified body is a "living way" is incomprehensible to a left-brain "reasonable" culture! I must never lose sight of PRAYER as an invitation to the realm of mystery. So it is that "reason" must yield to faith.

MAY THE SPLENDOR BE UNLOCKED.

FOUR

> "And after he had dismissed the crowds, he went up the mountain by himself to pray. When evening came, he was there alone,"
>
> **(Matthew 14:23)**

I am alone with Jesus.
I do not speak a word.
I send my heart to Him.
He shares His solitude with me.

MAY THE SPLENDOR BE REVEALED.

FOUR

"He said to them, "But who do you say that I am?"
(Matthew 16:15)

My desire is for the Lord.
Nothing more.
Nothing less.
This hallowed longing draws the gaze of
Jesus upon me.
His eyes are pools of LOVE.
They summon me to bathe in them.
I want to know JESUS.
I want to really know Him.
I want to communicate to
    JESUS WHO HE IS TO ME.

MAY THE SPLENDOR BE PROCLAIMED.

FOUR

"For this very reason, you must make every effort to support your faith with goodness, and goodness with knowledge, and knowledge with self-control, and self-control with endurance, and endurance with godliness, and godliness with mutual affection, and mutual affection with love. For if these things are yours and are increasing among you, they keep you from being ineffective and unfruitful in the knowledge of our Lord Jesus Christ." (2 Peter 1:5–8)

The channel between my thoughts and my
    heart, my heart and my thoughts is cleared.
These 8 seeds of the Kingdom begin to
    germinate in my SPIRIT—faith, goodness,
    knowledge, self-control perseverance,
    godliness, kindness, love.
My heart repeats them over and over again.
    My mind echoes my heart.
I see JESUS more and more and more.
He touches me with His smile.

MAY THE SPLENDOR SHINE.

FOUR

> "Take from among you an offering to the LORD; let whoever is of a generous heart bring the Lord's offering: gold, silver, and bronze; blue, purple, and crimson yarns, and fine linen; goats' hair, tanned rams' skins, and fine leather; acacia wood, oil for the light, spices for the anointing oil and for the fragrant incense, and onyx stones and gems to be set in the ephod and the breastpiece."
>
> **(Exodus 35:5–9)**

I am filled with humility.
Up to now I have NOT been "willing" to
    offer the
  LORD that which I wanted
    for mySelf,
In this moment I make an offering of
    EVERYTHING
PRECIOUS AND BEAUTIFUL in my life,
I see Calvary with new eyes. Fresh insight.
Is this all He could obtain with my treasure?
I REPENT.

MAY THE SPLENDOR BE RELEASED.

> **"Why have you forgotten us completely? Why have you forsaken us these many days?"**
> **(Lamentations 5:20)**

FOUR

My heart groans for African peoples.
My heart aches for the Church in Palestine.
He shows me the empty tomb.
We sit in SILENCE together.

MAY THE SPLENDOR HEAL THE WORLD.

FOUR

> **"Do you not know that in a race the runners all compete, but only one receives the prize? Run in such a way that you may win it. Athletes exercise self-control in all things; they do it to receive a perishable wreath, but we an imperishable one."**
> **(I Corinthians 9:24,25)**

My body becomes erect.
    SHE hears what is being said. DISCIPLINE.
The warfare of appetites heightens.
I invoke the NAME OF JESUS.
He "washes me with His word."
    (Ephesians 5:26)
   . . ."You are more than a conqueror."
                                       (Romans 8:37)

MAY THE SPLENDOR REIGN.

"I *am* a wall, and my breasts like towers: then was I in his eyes as one that found favour."
(Song of Solomon 8:10 KJV)

FOUR

He speaks my Name.
I rest upon His heart.
With His wounded hand, Jesus rubs my brow,
    my back, my feet.
I am Healed as He touches every wound
    and source of infirmity.
I am His.
He is Mine. Amen.

MAY THE SPLENDOR BREATHE INTIMACY.

FOUR

"The eye is the lamp of the body. So, if your eye is healthy, your whole body will be full of light;"
(Matthew 6:22)

I see JESUS.
With my heart. With my Soul. With my thoughts.
    With my eyes.
I SEE JESUS.
And my Body is filled with PEACE and LIGHT.
    LIGHT and PEACE.
JESUS is Reality.

MAY THE SPLENDOR ILLUMINE THE CHURCH.

"Be still, and know that I am God! I am exalted among the nations, I am exalted in the earth."
(Psalm 46:10)

FOUR

His POWER REIGNS.
I flow in the Life He ordained for me.
My obedience is effortless.
Anxiety departs from me.
Body and Soul I worship the LORD.

MAY THE SPLENDOR SHAPE MY POTENTIAL.

FOUR

> "The fear of the LORD is the beginning of wisdom; all those who practice it have a good understanding. His praise endures forever."
>
> (Psalm 111:10)

My heart belongs to the WORD of the
    LORD.
My SPIRIT also.
Opinion can no longer oppress me.
With strength of Heart I can love
    even those who do not love me.
May the LORD of Hosts be Glorified in my Life.
May the LORD of Eternity be Glorified in my Life.
May the LORD of Redemption be Glorified in my Life.

MAY THE SPLENDOR SET THE CAPTIVES FREE.

FOUR

> "For indeed the good news came to us just as to them; but the message they heard did not benefit them, because they were not united by faith with those who listened."
> (Hebrews 4:2)

I believe the Healing life of Jesus
    abides in me.
I believe the Liberating Spirit of Jesus
    prevails in me.
I believe the fire of Redeeming Hope burns in me.
I believe the Regenerating LIGHT of JESUS shines in me.
I believe the mercies of GOD pour out Refreshing in me.

MAY THE SPLENDOR BURST THE SEAMS OF TERROR.

FOUR

> "**May the God of peace himself sanctify you entirely; and may your spirit and soul and body be kept sound and blameless at the coming of our Lord Jesus Christ. The one who calls you is faithful, and he will do this.**"
>
> **(1 Thessalonians 5:23,24)**

Lord, Jesus CHRIST, Son of the LIVING GOD,
accomplish this word in my Life
NOW and FOREVER.
SANCTIFICATION and Peace
Come from Thee.
Let nothing in my PAST, PRESENT or
      FUTURE keep me from true HOLINESS.
      Amen.

MAY THIS SPLENDOR SHAPE THE UNIVERSE.

"GLORY be to the Father,
and to the Son
and to the Holy Ghost.
As it was in the
Beginning,
Is NOW and Ever
shall be.
World without End.
Amen.
Amen."

FOUR

FOUR

"Because you are precious in my sight, and honored, and I love you, I give people in return for you, nations in exchange for your life."

(Isaiah 43:4)

The UNSPOKEN movement in the SPIRIT energizes the Soul. Morning has come. My heart is light. My expectation in this day is of the LORD. I feel ALIVE. Isn't that remarkable! My very skin is aglow with NEW life.

I am learning that many words not only dissipate strength and disguise emptiness; but they also diminish LIGHT. What matters in being with the LORD *is* BEING WITH THE LORD. There is nothing that can be said—

"He speaks and the Sound of
HIS VOICE is so sweet
the birds hush
their singing."
(A.M.E.C. HYMNAL # 452)

Paul's Prayer that the Ephesians would "know the love of Christ that surpasses knowledge, so that you may be filled with all the fullness of God." (Ephesians 3:19) must be my Prayer for my own life. We take in so much that is unspiritual in our pursuit of religion that we soon have no room for GOD. This obscures the Light.

In the Unspoken world of prayer, I am gradually emptied of my emptiness and the **Inhabitation** of the SPIRIT of the LORD becomes a Reality. The manifestation is LIGHT, BEAUTY, GENEROSITY, JOY, LOVE and Health. To the undiscerning traveller; a smile in the form of a woman is sitting on the airplane. To the traditional religionist, an unconformed woman passes through the sanctuary breathing fire. To the ambitious, a woman of learning walks in regal anonymity. But the angels call me "precious." The ministering angels call me "precious." The Lips of Messiah whisper "PRECIOUS."

There is a beauteous splendor that encompasses the life of the Oblate. A LOVE Light Shines. She is the "Ray" of Hope that flickers in the valley of cynicism. The ruminations of her soul mirror the brilliance of the heavenlies. She walks in the LIGHT that she seeks.

The LIGHT is Prayer.
The LIGHT is Prayer.
The LIGHT over us is Prayer.

DANCE OF THE UNSPOKEN • 159

FOUR

The Soul of the Cojourner is designed for the unspoken. There is no word that accurately states What Light is. Yet the essence of Light pours out of every hymn that is sung. The intensity of LIGHT is witnessed at the miracle of every birth! And Light scatters darkness with every baptism. These are occurrences of the Soul. Stark realities of the Supernatural. Only in Spirit "talk" can one speak of "echoes" of LIGHT, "floods" of light, "tremors" of LIGHT. Because in our Soul life, we are susceptible to that which is beyond "knowing."

More and more, I am coming to glory in being the living space of GOD. More and more I sense the contours of my belief being re-shaped. It is the PRESENCE of Divinity that ignites my world and not the **sounds** of religion. And my Soul in love has been AWAKENED to God's Presence. In the Universe. In the Church. And in me.

The "Dance of the Unspoken" is to perfect **Inhabitation**. It is the season in which the treasures of the Kingdom are not mined. They are preserved, strengthened, secured. Not exposed to the elements. These jewels are kept only for the full view of the throne room. By prayer, I draw in fire so that they are refined, polished, glistening. My body becomes the habitat of the mysteries of God! The Soul force of the Kingdom reproduces itself in me by the Supernatural gift of Prayer. GOD has come to dance with me. Yet not a word is spoken!

FOUR — LIVING A NEW RHYTHMN

The SILENCE has taught me—
Every God-created,
 GOD-inspired presence
 is worthy of DIGNITY.
  RESPECT.
  ENCOURAGEMENT.
Let each one search her own SILENCE
 for HEALING SPACE.
  HEALING TIME.
  HEALING RELATIONSHIPS.
In SILENCE, let each one repossess the Gift of Imagination. It is the "magic" of GOD in human experience:
 Imagine and LIVE.
 Imagine and LOVE.
 Imagine and Heal the World.
In SILENCE, Imagination dissolves rigidities.
  OPENS THE SKY.
 Washes fatigue.
 HOPES the poor.
It is good for the SOUL to keep SILENCE.
 Silence is the reservoir of possibility.
 Silence nurtures RESISTANCE.
 Silence gives SIGHT.
Rediscover the SILENCE in your world.
 Where does it come from?
 Where does it go when it leaves you?
 Who shares it with you?
 For what can SILENCE be exchanged?
 At what price will you sacrifice it?
 For what reason have you given it away?
 Have you lost it?
  Where will you search for it?
   What will you do with it once you have found it again?
Have you discerned the SILENCE of GOD?

 The life shaped in SILENCE has meaning, POWER, virtue.
 Beloved,
  "Study to be quiet."
  LISTEN to the Silence of GOD.
  LISTEN and imagine.
  LISTEN and be Healed.
  LISTEN and be Renewed.

THE INVISIBLE APOSTOLATE

WRITE A PRAYER of HOPE for the NATIONS:

THE INVISIBLE APOSTOLATE   FIVE

"where then is my hope? Who will see my hope? Will it go down to the bars of Sheol? Shall we descend together into the dust?" (Job 17:15,16)

What is the Reality of a body flooded with HOPE?
Is it tremendous release?
Is it unfathomable serenity?
Is it joyous affirmation?
Is it relentless energy?
Does it feel like purple?
           or yellow?
              or aquamarine?
Does sunlight skip across your forehead?
Do moistures rise in dry places?
Does a heart made numb by desolation beat again?
Do shuffling feet pirouette?
Will the agonies of unconfessed failure depart?
Will my thoughts be saturated with possibility?
Will the nausea and weakness of anxiety disappear?
    WHO can say when HOPE will come?
    WHO can delay her arrival?
      . . . hasten her coming?
      . . . . ignore her Presence?
Is HOPE conceived, conferred, or caught?
ANSWER THIS:
What happens when God plants a kiss on a "natural" body?
Selah.

    Know this: the natural body is not beyond circumstances. Heat and Cold. Hunger and Thirst. Agony and the terror at midnight.
Leukemia.
Aids.
Muscular Dystrophy.
Ulcers.
Hemorrhage.
Rash.
Diabetes.
Stravation and
undiagnosed Death.

FIVE

But the sun "Also rises" is the retort of those who HOPE. Gethsemane is never far from the warlords,
the Pharisees,
the child molesters,
the gluttons,
status quo politicians,
the bankers,
intoxicated musicians,
church folk on tour,
death,
vultures,
hypocrisy,
spotless sanctuaries,
bird watchers or
"wailing women."
Just cross the street and you'll be there! Gethsemane. More a verb than a noun. Gethsemane. The noise is created by the SILENCE. The Silence of betrayal. The Silence of exhaustion. The Silence of arrested Hope. The moon walkers and fragile winged angels never enter the air space over GETHSEMANE. Too much traffic.

"I LOVE You," tears the heart out of the prostrate One. Wrecks the finances of the one who comes with a kiss. Gives a cock the power to bestow reckless insanity. Sends another fleeing NAKED! Brings us all to Calvary. It's Never far from Gethsemane!

So let the Dance begin.
The Father has chosen Redemption as His partner.
The disciples have each chosen fear.
Mary chose two other powerless women.
The only two that remain are JESUS and death.
What an intriguing couple they are! Surely, they will remain until the Dance has ended. Who knew it would last 3 days and through the nights? . . . . . And long after everyone else had gone away!?

This Dance is unrehearsed. Intense. A supernatural consummation. The HOST never comes forward. Remains in the background. Forever unseen, but Present. Of Course it is HOPE. Who else could communicate with such passion and skill?

THE INVISIBLE APOSTOLATE • 163

Let the CoJourner Consider:

How many steps in the Wilderness?
How many steps across the Red Sea?
How many steps to the pinnacle of Golgotha?
No one is counting.
No one remembers.
Manna is Hope.
Dry ground is Hope.
Resurrection is Hope.
Like the Wind.
No one can find its home.
Like the wind.
It moves by its own Power.
Like the wind.
It can be sudden and overpowering.
It can be gentle and refreshing.
Not many have prayed to HOPE.
For the *thing* HOPED FOR, Yes.
But not for HOPE itself.!
Perhaps this is the true Dance of the Spirit:
HOPE BRINGER TO THE NATIONS.
To Dance is to Hope.
To tease the laws of gravity
with Body Imaginations.
To Circle the Universe
with a gesture.
To Create Space in one movement.
And fan the flames of that "Strange Desire"—
HOPE.
To Dance is to HOPE.
To Dance is to Rise.
To Dance is to mount the Wind.

SELAH.

FIVE

"So they left the tomb quickly with fear and great joy, and ran to tell his disciples."

(Matthew 28:8)

FIVE

"For the Vision is yet for an
    appointed time;
But at the end it will speak,
    and it will not lie.
Though it tarries, wait for it;
Because it will surely come,
It will not tarry."
                              (Habakkuk 2:3)

That which our mothers glimpsed from a distance;
That which our fathers wept with GOD for in the anonymity of foreign midnights;
That which smoulders in the hearts of our youth as unreflective RAGE;
is not unknown to GOD.
    GOD shares in our sufferings with us,
        in our rejection with us,
        in our humiliation with us.
For the Redeemer of humanity says "in as much as you have done it unto the least . . . you have done it (also) unto me." (Matt. 25:40)
In the beginnings, we were designed to know GOD. The whole meaning of LIFE is purposed in attaining that irrefutable moment when the Soul proclaims, "I have SEEN THE LORD!"
Consequently, every oppression
          every violence
              every alienating reality that diminishes the human spirit
prolongs the agony of the Soul while corrupting our knowledge of GOD. And GOD suffers.
    An African Diasporic Spirituality empowers the Oblate to confront, transcend and transform the <u>cause</u> of our suffering. Make note of the 7 senses of a Diasporic Spirituality—

—A *sense* of AWE. African peoples do not compromise our reverence for the Sacred. The Holy. We Dance <u>unto</u> the LORD.

—A *sense* of History. African peoples as we WORSHIP maintain a ready reference to our GOD past as we open ourselves to our GOD future. We Dance <u>with</u> memory.

—A *sense* of Humor. African peoples make bold release while mocking the efforts of the devil with a therapeutic laughter. We make JOY when we Dance.

—A *sense* of Solidarity. African peoples understand that we are
    ONE with GOD
    one with creation
    one with all nations
    one with another.
    We are united in Dance.

—A *sense* of Color. African peoples express the vibrance, the energy, the force of the Spirit in our garments, liturgical art, ceremonies and pageantry. Our dancing is more vivid than subtle
                    pronounced than suggestive
                    explosive than passive.

—A *sense* of Rhythmn. African peoples house a multidimensional; many-faceted Spirituality of movement that embraces the cycles of life; the complexity of the mortal-immortal dialogue; and a Passion for the mystery. We dance to the heart beat of GOD.

—A *sense* of Expectation. African peoples believe when we gather to worship that GOD is *coming*;
When we kneel to pray—that GOD is *coming*;
When the word goes forth—that GOD is *coming*.
    We Dance to invoke GOD's spirit.
        to welcome GOD's presence.
        to praise GOD's Holiness.

By these 7 senses we are made strong in the LORD. Strong enough
    to endure
    to prevail
    to overcome
    to start again
    to Believe anyhow!
and to wait for GOD.

    "Because (the VISION) will surely come."

FIVE

FIVE

Dear Cojourner,

Are you lacking in any of your "senses"?

As you reflect upon your own spiritual formation, dialogue with others. PRAY Aloud. Look at the Life of your Spiritual teacher/s. and above all Dance!

I received confirmation in this regard during a season of sharing in Swaziland with Bishop Frederick H. Talbot (Guyana), his wife Dr. Sylvia Ross Talbot (Virgin Islands) and my husband, Bishop John R. Bryant (U.S.A.) For each of us, the power of a Diasporic Spirituality is personal as well as corporate; traditional and spontaneous as well as both mystical and liberating. Neither of us is ashamed to Dance. All of us long in prayer and witness for the liberation of African peoples,
the healing of the NATIONS,
and the JOY of the LORD.

Herein lies the HOPE of the Church—"All continued with one accord in prayer." (Acts 1:14) A Diasporic spirituality calls us beyond our suffering to creating new paradigms of resistance. A Diasporic Spirituality pursues the Christ of Faith outside the walls of Western legitimization. A Diasporic Spirituality comprehends the sovereignty of GOD and the integrity of African cultures. In Diasporic Spirituality woman is *also* "called"
"anointed"
"chosen"
"forgiven."

This gives us the POWER to HOPE.
the WILL to HOPE.
the sheer determination to HOPE.

HOPE creates the momentum for our transformation strategies. HOPE is an interdisciplinary,
intergenerational,
international,
inter-active FORCE.
INTELLIGENCE.
MOVEMENT.
LIFE.
REALITY.

Hope and shame can never live together. For where light IS, darkness must perish. There are so many streams of HOPE that flow in the life of the Oblate. Such REFRESHING. Such instantaneous Glory! Hope is the washing away of the stain of depression, sickness, loss, failure, emptiness. Even death. It sparks the Soul to prevail in adversity. What monumental encouragement awaits the one who seeks
BAPTISMAL,
EUCHARISTIC,
INTERCESSORY
or ETERNAL HOPE.
I must never allow discouragement to prevent me from Reclaiming any of the four. They are my inheritance in the LORD. My reservoir of HEALING joy.

When overwhelmed by negativity, I strain toward the music that HOPES and sing it LOUD. LOVE songs, Songs of overcoming, undiscernible SOUNDS of Passion. I drape myself in colors that HOPE—fuschia, purple, lime, coral and aquamarine. I drink Sparkling water. Write an erotic poem. Suggest subversion to my Soul. And PRAY for the Palestinian CHRISTIANS living under Israeli "apartheid." In the Supernatural, I wade in streams of HOPE.

Because Hell is real *and* on earth.

Let me remember and reflect. For what reason was I baptized? Was it the quantity of the water or the expectation of a mysterious inward change that motivated me? Did I merely "receive" the Holy Ghost? How far down in Sheol have I been plunged? If I stand up will I discover the waters are not that deep?

The movement from "victim" to self empowerment begins with the courage to interrogate one's reality. Assume nothing as permanent but the Grace of GOD. Spiritual Formation mandates that the Oblate inquire of her Faith. Dialogue with her belief. And Listen to God with her life. The Baptismal "candidate" is the recipient of a Spiritual Innocence. An Innocence that is victimized by scepticism/cynicism when worldly intercourse prevails. The HOPE of the Innocents will heal the world! Negativity is bondage. Doubt is crippling. Innocence is freedom! The freedom to expect the beautiful. To delight in simplicity. To enjoy the sight and touch of one's own body. To hear Doxologies in the movement of arms and legs, fingers and toes, head and neck. Undisturbed Innocence is a portrait of LOVE. Awe-inspiring. Comforting. Mysteri-

FIVE

"For you, O Lord, are my hope, my trust, O LORD, from my youth."

(Psalms 71:5)

BAPTISMAL

"Who can search out our crimes? We have thought out a cunningly conceived plot. For the human heart and mind are deep."

(Psalms 64:6)

FIVE

ous. To reclaim, bring forward, the Baptismal movement; is in special ways to be RESTORED to Innocence.

Perhaps the most tragic "side effect" of hopelessness is the death of imagination. This is not so for the Innocent! The Eye of the Innocent sees only possibility. "The glass is *always* half full!" The prayer life of Christians is Biblically Hoped and liturgically confirmed. If we would only pay attention, we would recognize that the rites of our faith are a wealth of GLORY. We might even discover that our HOPE is not so much sabotaged as it is unattended. There can be no Baptism *without* water. What is the meaning of these waters? Were my eyes closed or open? Was the white a symbol of a past reality or a sign pointing to a future revelation? How can "one baptism" have immortal consequences? Does it matter that I fear water?
                          cannot swim?
                 don't want my hair
                    "to go back?"
The Spiritual has gotten all tangled up with the natural. And HOPE can no longer *breathe*.

Then the LORD spoke to me:
    "I am with you to bless you and to keep you.
    Only don't run ahead of me. Don't be Afraid.
    Do not be easily provoked. Think no evil.
    Let LOVE prevail. The more I Bless you.
    The MORE and MORE LOVING you must
    be to all. Especially to those who
    have harmed you. LET MY LOVE ABIDE
    in YOU."

The "natural" in all things must be "subject" to the SPIRIT.
And so I pray to the LORD:

> "Return to me.
> Baptism return.
> The vows.
> The solemnity.
> The Holy privilege.
> The amazement." AMEN.

I want to reconnect with the IMMERSION. More LIGHT than fluid. More fact than symbol. More Fire than Ritual. I have been carried down—not by the mortal hands of the priest—but by the intransigence of a VOCATION that will not release me from its grasp. By the belief that I CAN be changed! The expectation that sin will NOT have the best of me. This is my **BAPTISMAL** HOPE. SIN shall not reign in my members. My Body, MIND, SOUL and STRENGTH shall be tabernacles of Holiness. I have been/am being/evermore shall be BAPTIZED. There are no waters too deep for me to walk on. I am immersed. I am *inwardly* changed. This is a SPIRIT and WATER and FIRE dance. Those who accuse me must step back. It's my turn NOW! There *is* air beneath the water. There is anointing oil mixed in the water. There are angels applauding at the bottom of the water. Until now, Only John the Baptist was "more than a prophet." And now I am MORE. More than a woman. More than a believer. More than a witness. MORE than flesh! Amen.

To this end I am baptized.

I am INWARDLY changed
 INITIATED INTO THE FAITH
 Proselyte of the Supernatural.
By this RITE, I have entered the REALM of the REIGN of GOD.
 THOSE who have gone before me, know that the way is HOLY. The undeclared will call me "HOLY." I die daily with Him, in Him, for Him. This is my desire and my vow. This is the Covenant of our LOVE.

FIVE

"Truly I tell you, among those born of women no one has arisen greater than John the Baptist; yet the least in the kingdom of heaven is greater than he."

(Matthew 11:11)

FIVE

"And baptism, which this prefigured, now saves you—not as a removal of dirt from the body, but as an appeal to God for a good conscience, through the resurrection of Jesus Christ,"

(1 Peter 3:21)

EUCHARISTIC

This is Baptism.

To be immersed in the awareness of the Redeeming death—life of Jesus CHRIST. Speaking only HIS words of consolation, Healing and Promise. Laying before Him like an infant ready to be changed by her Momma. Baptismal HOPE takes my Soul down in the waters of the Jordan with Jesus. I rise expecting to see heaven open in my life. Baptismal HOPE rings with the assurance that I belong to God and GOD is "pleased" with me. The intention is to make alive again. To bring refreshing. JOY restoration. To open the door of the heart for the Return of enthusiasm. Baptismal Hope can be inaugurated by the "laying on of HOLY hands," the anointing with oil or a consecrated Fast.

This is Baptism. When the "Ethiopian" in each of us pulls aside, searches the Scriptures, is taught by the Apostle, sees the water and pursues the change! To get "un-stuck" remember your Baptism and move on. It is the inauguration of your new identity! Another "side effect" of hopelessness is the loss of a *real* sense of identity. But once the Soul begins to Hope, you are on the path to the recovery of your own personhood. Sense of Self. Value. Esteem. Worth. You will begin to Dance again.

There is more. To the Oblate is also given **Eucharistic Hope.**
"As often as you shall
take this . . .
Do it in remembrance
of me." (Luke 22:19)

Eucharistic HOPE is the believer's **continual** opportunity for blessing. Each time I approach the table, I do so with an exhilarating contrition! In my unworthiness, I want/need to take this "body" and drink this "blood." I want/need the supernatural action of Calvary to take place *in* me. I want, I need the living sacrifice of JESUS CHRIST to penetrate me—

Mind, Soul, Body and emotion. Eucharistic HOPE is born of the remembering over and over and over again:
> I am LOVED.
> I am FORGIVEN.
> I am Redeemed.
> "It IS FINISHED." (John 19:30)
> Hallelujah.

EUCHARISTIC HOPE re-ignites covenant fires, re-confirms the gift of salvation, re-unites me with the very Body of Jesus CHRIST. This must be a fore-taste of Heaven! EUCHARISTIC HOPE re-stores the JOY of my Faith. My very body becomes host to the Host.

A mystery that the unbelieving will never fathom. A mystery that cannot be unraveled with taunting or mockery. As I reflect on "Holy Communion," I am again impressed by the simplicity of the elements—bread and wine. I am humbled by the magnitude of the LOVE. There on my knees, I am couched between the trauma of Calvary and the promise of the Resurrection. Eucharistic Hope calls me to live beyond the moment
> to see beyond the obvious
> to know beyond experience
> to love beyond gratification
> and to risk death!

Out of this HOPE, creativity is birthed, sustained and transformed. This is the Sacrament that the Artist must share often! It is the Sacrament of supernatural "balance"—pain and LOVE
> death and LIFE
> fear and Courage
> Self-centeredness and Generosity.
> natural and SPIRITUAL.

Let the Cojourner reflect upon the "Body" of Jesus Christ.
as Servant.
as Sacrifice.
as Sovereign.
Meditate on the "Blood" of Jesus Christ.
Atonement.
Healing.
New Covenant.
New Wine.
New Creation.

FIVE

There is HOPE for us.

It was " broken" that we might receive it.

"Poured out," that we might imbibe it. It serves no "natural" purpose. One can neither be filled or "satisfied" with it. It is barely a "taste." In fact it is more accurately a "hint," a "suggestion" of the Divine. Yet it is "sufficient" to keep the Church alive under communism, persecution, segregation, capitalism, exile, revolution, banishment, syncretism and tyranny! Rejection of Jesus has caused hopelessness to invade the Church of the 20th Century. A return to JESUS will assure the resurrection of HOPE. This Eucharistic Hope cannot be appropriated by any other deity. Nor will it accommodate the speculation of those who wish to manipulate theology to serve ideological purposes. JESUS CHRIST is LORD. This *is* the prevailing Reality of the Oblate. Those who are offended in this will never be seized by Eucharistic Hope. To "partake" is to be reconciled with others—friends, adversaries, strangers, "foreigners" and family members. To "partake" is to be united with the dead, the living and the unborn. It is to be made one with our former selves and our future Destiny. This is that great and mysterious centering moment when the Oblate is endued with the memory of Christ. And there is genuine Peace. This is our HOPE. And it is "beyond our comprehension." For this Peace is not a salty truce or a "demilitarized" zone or a "provisional" agreement. This Peace is of the New Kingdom—whose "architect and builder" is GOD. For a moment, we are "There." John, the Revelator saw it, Martin Luther King, Jr. saw it; but I have "tasted" it! And it's GOOD!

Come "HOPE" with me as we drink the wine and eat the loaf. "Remember" and be "filled." "Remember" and "rise" to your new position amidst the redeemed. The universe welcomes you home to HOPE. The very molecules of the universe are drenched in HOPE. A flailing hope must be nursed, set in the incubation of Prayer and Partake often of the Eucharist. HOPE revived, REVIVES!

> "Why are you cast down
> O, my Soul,
> Why disquieted within me?
> HOPE, thou
> in GOD." (Psalm 42:5)

INTERCESSORY

Don't stop now! There is a HOPE that is not uncommon to the believer—**Intercessory HOPE.** This too is glorious. When events, personalities or circumstance are not manifesting the LOVE of God; we

are not powerless observers or victims. We have active recourse to PRAYER. "The prayers of the righteous availeth much." (James 5:16) We know that through the Supernatural Realm, we gain entrance to All things. There is "no DISTANCE in GOD!" From our knees,
we can change the world,
influence decisions,
tear down strongholds,
transform lives,
heal the sick,
cast out devils,
impact the weather!
INTERCESSORY HOPE reminds us that we are 'Colabourers with CHRIST," that "the WORK IS ALL DIVINE," that "GOD is in Control." Most of all we see manifested that there IS POWER in Prayer. So much so that we are enabled to impart HOPE to others who knowingly *or* unknowingly must drink from the well of *our* faith.

As an Oblate, I am called to HOPE *for* others when their Faith is exhausted, will broken or dreams crushed. I am called to HOPE *with* others when their Vision is weighty, opposition strong and relentless, resources uncertain or health in crisis. The intercessor deposits HOPE in the Spirit of those for whom she prays. This is the work and worth of prevailing Prayer. Fasting on behalf of another. Prostrations in the place of another. Tarrying, wrestling, standing "in the gap" created by unbelief, warfare, disobedience, fear, discouragement or stress! The Oblate moves in the POWER of God to call down fire and raise UP Hope! Intercession may be done in secret, in union with others or as an act of Corporate liturgical Prayer. HOPE is undeniable proof of the power of INTERCESSION.

Let us make this our intention—to dismantle the infrastructure of violence in the supernatural realm. As we make our daily intercessions, let us not be passive concerning this the great enemy of HOPE.
> **"Holy Peace of Jesus Christ reign in the Universe. Expose and Rebuke the spirit of violence and Terror in the midst of the nations. Restore HOPE to all peoples. AMEN"**

The strength to Hope must come from intimacy with Jesus Christ and faithfulness to the Vision.

FIVE

FIVE

BODY SONG

"Do not be deceived; God is not mocked, for you reap whatever you sow." (Galatians 6:7)

HOPE makes all things new. Serenity declares my body to be Holy Land. The sanctuary of the unseen GOD, whose incarnating Song sets my Soul dancing. HOPE gives me the power to change mySelf. Hope bestows the gift to discern the presence of evil. Hope alerts me when I am being drawn out of the Realm of my Belonging. HOPE guides me in the mystery of Prayer. Reveals to me the MIRACLE of Life. Opens the way for me to be enthused with the Passion of GOD. Having journeyed so long in the "valley of the shadow of death;" I am surprised to meet myself in this Re-newed Body! And I am glad. A Body learning to HOPE is a peculiar experience. To unlearn patterns of sorrow. To dismantle phobias. To redesign my emotional response system. TO REST. To trust. To stop myself. To start over. To refuse to Run away (again).

To RELAX.
To RELAX.
To RELAX.
To RELAX.
To RELAX.
HOPE is breath.
IS SPIRIT.
IS LIFE.
HOPE is GOD.

> Idolatry cannot produce HOPE.
> Philosophy will not sustain HOPE.
> Defeat will never kill HOPE.
> HOPE is the Spirit of GOD. ALIVE
> and in Me.

WRITE an Affirmation that will reproduce itself as HOPE in your life:

THE INVISIBLE APOSTOLATE • 175

BELOVED COJOURNER;
The past cannot be changed or duplicated. I grant myself clemency from my former lives. Spirit moves. Spirit REIGNS. Spirit Heals. Spirit informs. I am the one who bears witness to this Apostolate. I am the one who shuddered in the prison of Anxiety. I am released on the recognizance of the Holy Ghost. Cross the tracks quickly my Soul! Leave barren images on the other side. Nature takes its course and a great heaving permeates the NATIONS. My shoulders ache from the burden of prophecy. There is Sabbath Rest and I seek it. (If I wear eye shadow the color of peridot, they cannot see through to my Soul and steal the LIGHT.)
  "Foolish Woman of Kente Cloth
have you no wisdom?"
I left the path.
When I sought "approval."
I left the path.
When the jewels
of culture were flaunted and I desired them!
I left the path.
When the Rains came.
I own now my peculiar Destiny. My incredible Dance.
The movement begun in the Spirit is by the Spirit sustained.
In consecrated beginnings,
lesser gods die.
The LIGHT of GOD rises shining. Shining.
Shining all over me.
Shining within me.
The LIGHT shines.
Shining forth HOPE to the Nations. SHINING.
SHINING.
SHINING bright with atonement.
Shining Justice.
Shining Glory.
Shining Truth.
I am in the LIGHT.
The LIGHT is before me.
Darkness must flee.
I am the LIGHT.
I am RADIANT.
MY BODY sings, "GLORY!"
My Body sings, "GLORY!"

FIVE

"Therefore, while the promise of entering his rest is still open, let us take care that none of you should seem to have failed to reach it."

(Hebrews 4:1)

"Prize her highly, and she will exalt you; she will honor you if you embrace her."

(Proverbs 4:8)

"Therefore my heart is glad, and my soul rejoices; my body also rests secure."

(Psalms 16:9)

"...and the glory of the Lord rises upon you."

(Isaiah 60:1)

FIVE

As we reflect upon the movements of the Holy Spirit.
As we pay attention to our lives.
As we listen to our experiences.
As we study our relationships.
We are being taught.
These contemplative and experiential lessons directly impact our strength to HOPE.

Perhaps you will draw from our 7 pedagogical episodes Hope meanings that will bring clarity and focus to your own journey.

Perhaps you will "learn" that there is another more risking path for you to take.

Perhaps you will find yourself dancing again!

The "Dancing Church" must HOPE for the POOR.
                WITH THE POOR.
                AS THE POOR.
The dance of the Church must warn the nations.
                defend the children.
                Watch for GOD.
                Rebuke the devourer.
                Celebrate Life.
                Heal the sick.
                Invoke Justice.
                Demonstrate LOVE.
Being "taught" by the Spirit to HOPE, my Soul
counsels my thoughts on the fear of lack in a
materialistic world culture; cautions me
of the danger of fatigue, and guides me to
a fresh awareness of the Presence of GOD.

This is the source of HOPE's power
of REFRESHING: "Emmanuel"—God is with US.
GOD is truly with us. The poor do not Dance
alone. We dance with GOD unchaperoned!

There are threads of HOPE in what
appears as an "ordinary" day/
                relationship/
                experience.
With these threads, we shall weave a new world VISION.

PEDAGOGIES OF HOPE

Woman in Waiting:
Sometimes I sit here waiting.
Believing that heaven has emptied
    herself in me. WAITING.
Believing that time has been eclipsed by
    Beauty. WAITING.
Believing that the sun cloud has hidden
    the face of God from all desperados
    and evildoers.

When I wait, I remember the long morning heaven loaned to me so that love could call me back from the dead. And so I danced my way out of fatigue and into exhilaration. Before when I was afraid to PRAY/Dance. I would turn on the television which rendered me numb and senseless. I would then orchestrate my presence in the world to the pleasure of a digital clock. The Dance/PRAYER within would rage and torment my body which became dis-eased by the impact of it all. I became sterile, frigid. Unable to respond or conceive. God gave me a warning. "Do not throw flesh after SPIRIT." God gave me a vow. "As I was with Moses so I will be with you." God gave me a prophecy. "We shall speak with ONE voice." God gave me a vowel. "Y." God gave me the peridot stone. The symbol of the presence and Power of Healing. How long had GOD been waiting?

                    SELAH

FIVE

I

"Hope deferred makes the heart sick, but a longing fulfilled is a tree of life."

                (Proverbs 13:12)

FIVE **II**

> "He said to them, "Because of your little faith. For truly I tell you, if you have faith the size of a mustard seed, you will say to this mountain, 'Move from here to there,' and it will move; and nothing will be impossible for you. Howbeit this kind goeth not out but by prayer and fasting."
>
> (Matthew 17:20,21)

From my window, I look out upon the Detroit River. Like my soul, it flows along uninterrupted. Then something in nature/history causes it to divide
    within itself.
Only to reunite at a point down stream. Has the season of separation changed its nature?
    altered its Purpose?
    Reformulated its Direction?
    Brought strength?
        weakness?
        Imagination?
Do the waters live in expectation of a new solidarity?
Is it now more of a RIVER?
Had the water lost its' identity?
What message is in the convergence?
            Providence,
            Fate,
            Volition,
            Nature?
Hope that rests in the unopposed FLOW must give birth
    to itself when that FLOW is interrupted.
GOD is in the waters.
GOD is in ME.
    Though the waters divide and separate, GOD remains one.
    When I am in my own experience distanced from mySelf; In CHRIST, I am ONE.
Therefore, I am continuously reaching
    into LIFE in search of MYSELF—
    the greater UNITY.
HOPE is the consistent, unbroken FLOW.
HOPE is GOD.
GOD is HOPE.
HOPE calls to me, like the RIVER.
The movement of GOD is the impulse of HOPE.
Going from mystery to Eternity.
Breathing dreams and Visions into the sleepless
    nights of the forgotten poor.
Sweeping up villages in the Path of a storm with His right hand.
Fanning mustard seeds through refugee camps.
HOPE terrifies the devil!

There are ships passing on the River.
They are *not* the River.
Birds scoop down on the River.
They are not the River.
There is a bridge that crosses the River.
The bridge is not the River.

I am a bird.
I am a ship.
I am a bridge.
I am a RIVER.
SELAH.

FIVE

FIVE · III

"It is the spirit that gives life; the flesh is useless. The words that I have spoken to you are spirit and life."

(John 6:63)

"The LORD, your God, is in your midst, a warrior who gives victory; he will rejoice over you with gladness, he will renew you in his love; he will exult over you with loud singing"

(Zephaniah 3:17)

You can *actively* receive the deposit of HOPE that comes to you by the HOLY SPIRIT present in the WORD of GOD: "Therefore my heart is glad, and my soul rejoices; my body also rests secure." (Psalms 16:9) *Feel* your body respond. *Experience* the impact of HOPE. Continuous hopelessness breeds disease, infirmity, sickness, powerlessness! As you begin to HOPE, refreshing comes.
       enthusiasm comes.
       health comes.
       optimism comes.

HOPE is not final. HOPE is ever incomplete! HOPE is born and fed and shaped by every life experience. Depression is a matter of the Body Soul clamoring to HOPE again! Once HOPE is glimpsed/tasted/echoed/ignited—

 I am compelled to get UP.
      to get OUT.
      to **move** mySelf.

The end of the desert is one step (after another) away!

 Beloved Cojourner begin now to **welcome** the Spirit of HOPE into your life.

 Breathe in HOPE.
 Breathe OUT despair.
 Breathe in HOPE.
 Breathe OUT anxiety.
 Breathe in HOPE.
 Breathe OUT disease.
  In the Name of JESUS.

In the ordinariness of our days and nights, it is possible to be without HOPE and NOT realize it. In subtle ways anticipation slips from us. Enthusiasm is exchanged for security. Imagination is replaced by protocol. But as one prays to HOPE—that strange DESIRE—one's life becomes anchored in the SPIRITUAL. The natural realm can only "imitate" HOPE. Authentic HOPE is a matter of the SPIRIT. This is why one patient outlives the prognosis and another with the same infirmity dies at the very announcement! HOPE is SPIRIT fire. SPIRIT power. SPIRIT force. Trace your STEPS Back to your HOPING GROUND. Set up your Tent. Live THERE!
       SELAH.

IV   FIVE

FIVE

V HOPE is that which precedes
                penetrates
   and remains when chaos has dissipated.
It is the joy at conception,
   the nausea during morning sickness,
   the laboring agony,
   and the momentous birth!
HOPE is a living Spirit in search of a body,
                    an imagination,
                    a courageous will.

To be an Oblate there is an incarnating moment, when I make the decision to trust that GOD had something beautiful in mind when GOD created me. That GOD has something Holy in mind concerning the NATIONS. And that GOD has not abandoned the CHURCH.

   "Be vigilant my SOUL!
   Lest the powers of negation
   overwhelm my desire
   to HOPE.

   Be awake my SOUL!
   Expell the shadows of evil
   that encroach upon
   my passive memory.

   Be forever in Song my Soul!
   As new beginnings continue
   to sup with me and strengthen me
   on my Journey toward being whole."
                              AMEN

A hopeless woman leaves God weeping!
A hopeless nation takes God's breath away!
A hopeless church tears to shreds the heart of heaven!
But a solitary Oblate by the power of HOPE can
rise to her Destiny, liberate the Church,
heal the world and bring Glory to GOD!
                    SELAH.

FIVE **VII** A prevailing sense of inadequacy and unworthiness can be the torment of a life of Oblation IN THE WORLD. There is no escape! Not even the cloister is safe, immune, care-free. The controversies of human experience in the culture, in the church and within one's own personality are ever present. It is helpful to recall what helps you to HOPE.

A sound?
A sight?
A touch?
A person?
A passage?
An experience—REST. A MEAL. A WALK. Playing with a child?
What "helps" you to HOPE?
Perhaps, it might be easier to reflect upon how you "help" others to HOPE!
There is no better way than to ask!

Dear Cojourner;
The following encounters are intended to teach us something incredible about HOPE. To call us *out* of our familiar emotional ground. To teach us new language. To compel us to discover the breadth of our humanity. HOPE changes the OBLATE, the CHURCH and the NATIONS. It is both solitary and Cosmic. LET HOPE teach us to LISTEN: to others, to GOD, to our bodies! LISTEN and LEARN. LEARN and LIVE, LIVE *in* HOPE!

THE INVISIBLE APOSTOLATE • 185

FIVE

These 4 pages are dedicated to learning from others what brings them HOPE. DO NOT TREAT THIS LIKE AN ACADEMIC "ASSIGNMENT." Give yourself and others time and space to experience the process. If you are *not* ready; go on to page 189 and return to this segment when it is comfortable for you to do so. As I LISTEN, I pray to the LORD to teach me what life response the Holy Spirit requires of me:

A child under 12   Date _____

Lesson for ME:

Someone of a different Race   Date _____

Lesson for ME:

FIVE A Clergywoman Date _____

Lesson for ME:

Someone LIVING in Poverty Date _____

Lesson for ME:

A Senior Citizen Date _____ **FIVE**

Lesson for ME:

A "Successful" Personality Date _____

Lesson for ME:

FIVE   An Incarcerated Person   Date _____

Lesson for ME:

A Family Member   Date _____

Lesson for ME:

"Now GOD,
I pray EVEN NOW,
for my precious Cojourner.
I pray in the POWER of the
NAME of JESUS.
I pray in the REALITY
of the ANOINTING on my own life.
Bless Your people.
Bless Your people.
Bless Your people.
Let HOPE arise in every cell of our bodies.
Let HOPE arise in every oppressive predicament.
Let HOPE arise in the controversies of the nations.
HEALING HOPE.
LIBERATING HOPE.
RECONCILING HOPE.
REVELATION HOPE.
You, LORD are the GOD who HOPES for us.
You, LORD establish the ground of our HOPE
   in Your WORD.
By the power of the RESURRECTION of JESUS from
   the Dead, may HOPE
     NOW abide in us,
     with Thee,
     FOREVER.
        AMEN"

FIVE

FIVE

I recognize the importance of sustaining the HOPE within me.
It is so easy to accomodate the move of a non-specific spirituality. But when I consider JESUS, my HOPE is set ablaze! There is nothing *outside* me that compares with the unfathomable Gift *within* me.

As I sit here, I am praying the LORD to raise up INTERCESSORS who in the *NAME of JESUS* will restore HOPE to the NATIONS, the Church and families.

I am praying the LORD to call out HOLY WOMEN who have the power to discern the cloaked evil that has set upon African peoples and in the *NAME of JESUS* expose it and *rebuke it*!

I am praying the LORD to HOPE me as I go forth in the *NAME OF JESUS* and that the LOVE of GOD and the Favor of the LORD will abound toward me richly!

    My HOPE *is* to GLORY in the LORD.
    My HOPE *is* to see the Kingdom of God manifested
        on earth as it *is* in heaven.
    My HOPE *is* that the true Chruch will rise
        as a STAR in the NIGHT.
    My HOPE *is* in the LORDship of JESUS CHRIST.

TO THE COJOURNER:
    It is an act of encouragement to NAME your HOPE.
        To speak it LOUD.
        To SING it.
        To BATHE in it.
        To WALK with it.
        To Dance to it.
        To EMBODY your HOPE.
        To Spell it in your sleep.
        To NAME it to a Stranger.
        To Whisper it to your Soul.
        To wait with it for SUNRISE.
        To Believe that in it you will never be Ashamed!

"Uphold me according to your promise, that I may live, and let me not be put to shame in my hope."

(Psalms 119:116)

FIVE

The Spirit of God is the PASSION in Hope. This SPIRIT, when I reach out to others for rescue; draws me to the LIGHT *within*. Back to the LIGHT. The place of Eternal Belonging.
The matchless cresendo of HOPE.
Overflows.
Overpowers.
Negation is transformed.
Healed by the LIGHT within.
God's "magic" is the "fun" experienced as irrespressible JOY.
Shameless.
Guilt FREE.
Beauty.
Honesty.
I now TRUST what I LOVE.
Believe in WHO I LOVE.
Celebrate, and Expose my "Self" LOVE.
    Let us Pray.
"Love Eternal.
    Wonder that cannot be quantified.
    Brilliance of all Celestial intentions;
    Power that Fathoms the OCEANS;
I delight in CHRIST in me.
    Resonating with the Universe;
    Awakened to the unspoken sounds of the lonely;
    Dying to LIVE again.
LET ME BE YOUR PLEASURE.
    Build arks on dry land.
    Provide a space for all creation.
    Summon my family to a living FAITH.
    Captivate the Church with the imagination of GOD.
And sleep in the HOPE of the
    Resurrection.
                                 Amen.

FIVE

"I am going to send an angel in front of you, to guard you on the way and to bring you to the place that I have prepared. Be attentive to him and listen to his voice; do not rebel against him, for he will not pardon your transgression; for my name is in him. But if you listen attentively to his voice and do all that I say, then I will be an enemy to your enemies and a foe to your foes."

(Exodus 23:20–22)

HOPE restores and sustains a sense of "connection."

She does not Dance Alone who has learned to Pray. The Holy One said to me, "Zohar, *your* angel is with you." I am thankful. Although I have known of my supernatural companion, I did not know His/Her Name. I am never bereft of a Cojourner. One who watches over me and defends me when I pray. Thank God! "God, thank YOU."

The Church has been so wounded by "natural" ways. It makes it appear that God is a failure! Invoke the Name of JESUS. Interrogate your reality with the NAME of Jesus. Only then can we discern the hopelessness *in* the churches. Let us welcome Jesus to the Church again. In our hearts. In our Songs. Let us make Him welcome.

**Lord Jesus CHRIST,
I welcome You.
I welcome You.
As friend.
I welcome You.
As LORD.
I welcome You.
As Messiah.
I welcome You.
Come NOW.
Come NOW.
Into my thoughts.
Come NOW.
Come NOW.
Into my Heart.
Do come LORD Jesus
and REIGN
in my SOUL.
REIGN FOREVER
in my SOUL.
Amen.**

The sheer intangibility of HOPE defies mortal opposition. Solitary resistance is contagious. The Oblate as "exemplar" births a new generation of protégeés.

Covenant Life must be restored, if HOPE is to reign. Spiritual disasters are crying out to us to evacuate the culture and flee to higher ground. It will be safe there. We will love Holiness better than LIFE. This is how we know that our HOPE is sure. Certainly We are not the Rainbow generation. (Genesis 9:12,13) There will be no sign in the heavens to confirm our election. A mere Consolation of Soul is the token we long for. HOPE knows that I am not alone. Though the lights go out in the city. And the choirs are disbanded for want of a director. Though the economy swallows up my finances. Though the saints mock me and scorn. Though injustice hogs the road on a two-way street. Though seminarians still ask the question—"WHO IS GOD?" Even when going to church has become a bore. And attending banquets a comedy and a delusion. I will say to my SOUL, "Let US Dance!"

Because HOPE for me is not a matter of church membership. I have come to know JESUS—experience His Presence and POWER—both within and beyond the walls of the denomination. To actively, actually *KNOW* that we *are*, in fact, "GOD's PEOPLE." I have endured not having a nation of my own, because my GOD who loved the Universe into being has placed me in "an open space." I have been awakened by the broken hearts of African peoples crying through the generations for a NEW DAY. And then I arise to face the Wind. It is heavy with the scent of apocalypse. I recognize that it will *not* be as long as it has been! In that moment, the spirit of Jeremiah speaks to me:

> ". . . The LORD will create a new thing
> on earth—
> a woman will surround a man."
> (Jeremiah 31:22)

FIVE

"This is the covenant that I will make with the house of Israel after those days, says the Lord: I will put my laws in their minds, and write them on their hearts, and I will be their God, and they shall be my people."

(Hebrews 8:10)

"Ephphatha."

(Mark 7:34)

FIVE

INTERCESSION

This is the Dance of Prophecy. When the Holy Spirit comes and rests upon me with a vocabulary that dismantles the infrastructure of TERROR that has razed the HOPE of a people ridiculed by the nations; exploited by religious demagogues and forgotten by the musicians.

This Dance of Prophecy comes to every generation. God is highly exalted in the life of one who makes no claim upon things as they are. One who steps out of the tabernacle of fear and leaps into the freedom of Revelation. Surrounded by LOVE. By LOVE made whole. Endued with LOVE. She speaks in the Power of the Godhead. Her prayings exorcise the priesthood. The squalor created by bad religion is exposed! Condemnation has lost its' power. The siege is over. Revelation comes dancing!

DANCING.
DANCING.
DANCING.

NO PRAYER has been prayed with such LIGHT. With such Self-abandonment. With such power of HOPE. By the same prophetic spirit, I am rendered a compassionate INTERCESSOR for the NATIONS.

If I speak to the people of the Kingdom of GOD; shall I not also speak to the LORD concerning the people? Intercession dissolves the feelings of powerlessness that attend a view of the world as it appears to be. Intercession brings in sight the not-visible realities that are at work in the heart of GOD and in the Soul Life of GOD's people.

Dear CoJourner,
Pray for the Holy SPIRIT in revelation
to come to you in all HOPE,
Godly PASSION and LIBERTY of Soul.
SELAH.

A window has been installed above the SKY that I can see through when I DANCE/PRAY. This is the work of HOPE. HOPE put it there. I must teach the nations to dance again.
LIFE in the beginnings is Dance.
The flow of the Eternal is persistent.
One generation is joined to the next in Hope.
Hope is God's defiance of the obvious in a consenting vessel.
Hope is the wonder that draws the unborn from
    their hiding places when humanity has lost its
    capacity to dream.
Hope is an ocean of miracles when all that is
    needed is one mustard seed.
Hope ignites Passion in the dying to live another Day.
HOPE dances in the heart of the mute who pens
    the WORD that gives VOICE to the nations.
HOPE laughs when reluctant Priests prepare a
    Requiem for the condemned.
HOPE is an affair of the Soul.

BAPTISMAL HOPE TRANSFORMS.
    This is the strength of the Oblate.
EUCHARISTIC HOPE RENEWS.
    This is the integrity of the Church.
INTERCESSORY HOPE LIBERATES.
    This is the power of the nations.

FIVE

*"For with you is the fountain of life;
in your light we see light."*

(Psalms 36:9)

"When the wicked die, their hope perishes, and the expectation of the godless comes to nothing."

(Proverbs 11:7)

FIVE   **ETERNAL**

"in the hope of eternal life that God, who never lies, promised before the ages began—"

(Titus 1:2)

"It is sown a physical body, it is raised a spiritual body. If there is a physical body, there is also a spiritual body."

(1 Corinthians 15:44)

"For since we believe that Jesus died and rose again, even so, through Jesus, God will bring with him those who have died."

(1 Thessalonians 4:14)

Finally, there is another HOPE that is unfathomable to the unbeliever. This is **ETERNAL HOPE**. The most significant HOPE available to humanity. The delusion of finitude is that it is every where and pertains to all things. How often have we heard it rumored: "nothing is forever." With such we bid farewell to childhood, friendship, marriage, wealth, privilege, happiness, fidelity, beauty, health and even religion. But look again! This time more deliberately. This time without ulterior motives or rationalizations. "Forever" is within us. Let it flow freely. Let FOREVER and all its beauty seep into our conversations. Our lovemaking. Our worship. Our Silence. This FOREVER has the POWER to face down sickness, betrayal, chaos and even death.

My Body needs to Know this.
My Body awaits this assurance.
My Body sings in the arms of my
    Eternal HOPE.
My Body exults at the prospect that
    I will dance FOREVER.
This is Eternal Hope.

To know that when Christ comes again, He will "receive me unto Himself." To know that LIFE in Christ does not ultimately give place to death! To realize that the sins of my body and against my body have been the work of death. **But I have a body reality beyond the historical!**

Under the tutelage of the culture, Infirmity and ethnicity have done a Cruel work on the body image of mothers and their daughters for generations. Unable to see Divinity expressed in our mortal bodies; we did harm to ourselves and allowed others to. We rejected our own bodies. It is kingdom irony that our "Eternal" Hope compels us to look again at our "natural" bodies. To celebrate the intricacies, contours, rhythms and tones of this miracle—incarnation. Spirit alive in the Flesh!

Eternal HOPE compels me to put my life in focus. I can then measure EVERYTHING by Eternity. There are only three priorities in Eternity:
> HOW I LOVE GOD.
> HOW I LOVE OTHERS.
> HOW I LOVE MYSELF.

The fundamental issue being how I *receive* and *Respond* to the LOVE of GOD.

Mortal setbacks lose their sting in the embrace of the Eternal. What is my Eternal Hope and that of every person who has consented to the LORDship of Jesus CHRIST? The magnitude of my presence on the planet cannot be restricted by the culture. The impact of my life and life work are not even subject to my own volition or death. The *"appearance"* of success or failure are not Kingdom criteria. For God, the sole issue is "faithfulness." For the "Faithful," Eternal HOPE brings serenity, Grace, triumph and the favor of the LORD.

Therefore, HOPE cannot be driven, superimposed, mandated or asserted. People must be LOVED into HOPE. The Soul conceives HOPE in the darkness of prevailing prayer. The SOUL is taught to HOPE by following the sparks of testimony on the paths of the martyrs and saints. That SOUL lives in HOPE whose doxologies rid the heart of bitterness, unforgiveness and self-reproval. HOPE is gentle but unafraid. HOPE lives beyond the reach of covetousness and on the grounds of compassion. To HOPE is to trust the Silence of GOD and the paradox of LOVE. That suffering is inevitable. Yet, HOPE shines.

**WRITE A FOUR LINE SONG
of HOPE for the CHILDREN
of the WORLD:**

FIVE

"but in your hearts sanctify Christ as Lord. Always be ready to make your defense to anyone who demands from you an accounting for the hope that is in you;"

(1 Peter 3:15)

FIVE

"My tears have been my food day and night, while people say to me continually, "Where is your God?""

(Psalms 42:3)

"you have wrapped yourself with a cloud so that no prayer can pass through."

(Lamentations 3:44)

As I write through tears of love-pain, I understand that my HOPE must be in GOD ultimately and always. "Well meaning" cojourners and an assemblage of "good intentions" cannot go the DISTANCE. I must position mySelf in PRAYER. Emotion being a powerful gift to humanity; I pay homage to my feelings. Respect them and move ON. I must MOVE ON. HOPE stands me back on my feet again. I must MOVE ON. Commitment is a word that my people have not yet learned to spell. I must move on. By the POWER of the Holy SPIRIT and in the flames of the LOVE of God; I shall be taught. Then, I shall teach! The anointing dances upon the cloud. And the cloud covers me.

By day. By night. I am being shaped by HOPE. The impulse of "flight" is losing its momentum. HOPE is a deep and burning fire. "Come LORD Jesus, Come Quickly," I pray in the tumult. The sensory evidence when I awaken is PEACE, gentle peace. I am where I have been. But something more attends my thoughts. My Being. It must be HOPE!

Those who witness from the bottom of Eternity are those who must be HOPED. It is impossible to see the cohesion of LIFE from there. The voice of the future is muddled by the walls of the abyss. Those who get out do not return. The stench is overpowering. The churches cannot long endure it. LIGHT is an apocalyptic occurrence. John the Baptist has been beheaded! Any other martyrdoms go unnoticed. No one knows it's Sunday morning. The ecology of despair obscures the break of day. Yet, from a distance, someone can be seen dancing. Dancing out of a TOMB. Robed only in LIGHT, but dancing. Dancing out of a TOMB. Surrounded by SILENT THUNDER. Yet Dancing. Dancing OUT of a TOMB. With an entourage from the heavenlies. Dancing out of a TOMB!

    It is breathtaking.
    So is HOPE.
    It is awe-inspiring.
    So is HOPE.
    It is Supernatural.
    But then, so is HOPE!

FIVE

From a distance, I come to recognize the futility of politics. The vanity of reason. And the emptiness of "good will." There is only ART and PRAYER. These are the purveyors of HOPE. (Yes, there is SONG. I know this. But when we pray, it is merely the soul singing!)

One can return to the tomb and await the Dancer's encore. Or one can join the Dance wherever you are. Without trumpets of thunder or light from the heavenlies. ONE can still Dance. No applause from the angels. Without throngs of well wishers. Still, I can Dance. There are no orchestral accompaniments at the bottom. But the music of HOPE emanates from the strings of a believer's heart.

> And I can dance, dance, dance, all NIGHT.
> Dance in the Dark.
> Dance on the burning Sand.
> Dance to my own music
> DANCE all by myself.
> And Dance right out of this TOMB.
> Hallelujah.

Consider these things when tempted to give up—
> "It is good that one should wait quietly for the salvation of the LORD."
>
> (Lamentations 3:26)

> "But if we hope for what we do not see, we wait for it with patience."
>
> (Romans 8:25)

> "Therefore prepare your minds for action; discipline yourselves; set all your hope on the grace that Jesus Christ will bring you when he is revealed."
>
> (1 Peter 1:13)

FIVE

This is the ONE light that I wish to share with all peoples at all times. It is HOPE. It is the reason I keep oil for my lamp, bring barrels of water to Cana, Lay hands on the sick, batik the dreams of the dysfunctional. Hope moves me.

> in me.
> through me.
> with me.
> for me.
> about me.

I had feared to HOPE, so I would not PRAY. **(Selah.)**
And now that I HOPE, I can also PRAY. (Selah)
There is neither Rage nor Rancor in HOPE. Even Terror must give place to HOPE. The conscious awareness of the moving of my own body excites me to hope. A Holy Adrenaline sets FIRE to my imagination. And my body begins to remember herself before she died. Hope destroys the myths of the subconscious. Makes virile the life I never owned. As Passion bursts the seams created by rejection, ridicule, mockery and betrayal; I consent to this power within me. Now I can fly! No longer a "broken-winged bird" as Langston described.
I have HOPE.
To pray is to HOPE.

WHY NOT PEN A THREE-WORD PRAYER OF HOPE?

AMEN.

A dancer caught in the traffic of the ordinary can either suffocate
or Fly.
I choose to Fly.
How perilous the flight taken without Hope.
I choose to fly.
To dance is to Fly.
To PRAY is to DANCE.
Every hymn is a Journal of HOPE. Every resistance to the tyranny of the ordinary makes HOPE alive. This is what helps me to Hope:
the smell of baby oil.
a picture of Harriet Tubman.
the sounds of Sweet Honey on the Rock.
the sight of Thema dancing.
the feel of sand in ocean water between my toes.
an empty sanctuary at dusk.
a gift of Rosary beads.
Marvin Gaye singing "What's Goin On?"
The LORD'S PRAYER.
My son Jamal.
Asata smiling.
You see, Hope is not the fruit of incantation.
It is the work of the Holy Spirit in the prayer life of the immortal Soul. I will no Longer occupy the seat of the VICTIM passively awaiting the arrival of my executioners. I shall arise. Infirmity, poverty, depression, duplicity, slander will have to pursue me. Thank God, "goodness and mercy" are following me as well! Hallelujah.
Hope is experiencing clear water travelling down my parched throat before I ever reach the well.
Hope appears dormant until awakened by adversity. And then every

FIVE

"At that moment the curtain of the temple was torn in two, from top to bottom. The earth shook, and the rocks were split. The tombs also were opened, and many bodies of the saints who had fallen asleep were raised."

(Matthew 27:51,52)

FIVE

cell in my body is regenerated by this inauspicious intruder.
Heavenly portion.
Supernatural deposit.
Healing medicine of the LIGHT.
Now that death has been expunged from my memory; my body delights with every Life flirtation. Angels nibble on my ear. Play with my toes. Rub my brow. And wrap their wings around my waist. I am never Alone. I will not die again! The power of GOD exudes a tranquil Grace when LOVE stands still. I have wanted more and more for the refugees of my desire to return to the Village I call home: **Prayer**. The fences have been taken down. The abandoned garden is being tilled, fertilized and watered. The lake of Revelation is so very clear. The horizon is endless.

Come home to me misty desire.
Come home to me sacred loom.
Return, oh Spirit of Light.
Return.
Return to me, oh Innocence.
Patience, return and live in me.
Simplicity, Come.
Transparency, Come.
Gentleness return unto me.
Affection, so far from home.
Return.
Teach me again
to respond to your promptings
Help me again to
Imagine with GOD.
To envision a world
filled with the laughter
of children.
Teach me strength.
Teach me compassion.
Let me not be
AFRAID or
Ashamed to

speak those three terrifying words:
"I Love you":
to relations,
antagonists,
soul mates,
and critics.
dictators,
healers,
children and
all dancers.
Talk to my body again
about touching
and embracing
and personal
benedictions.
Dear affection only you
can turn on the
light in my
heart.
Come Home.
Won't you PLEASE
Come
Home."

Amen.

FIVE

"For now we see in a mirror, dimly, but then we will see face to face. Now I know only in part; then I will know fully, even as I have been fully known."

(1 Corinthians 13:12)

FIVE

For in hope we were saved. Now hope that is seen is not hope. For who hopes for what is seen?"

(Romans 8:24)

"On that day his burden will be removed from your shoulder, and his yoke will be destroyed from your neck. He has gone up from Rimmon,"

(Isaiah 10:27)

This apostolate has the advantage of invisibility. The enemy cannot see HOPE coming. Cannot monitor her progress. Make contract with her assassin. Because the thing conceived to destroy her—nourishes her instead. Distraction brings her FOCUS. Detractors win allies for the VISION. HOPE is the deposit of the Supernatural. Having its origins in the heavenlies; it cannot be seduced by natural gratification. GOD is in HOPE's beginnings. Her conception, maturation and fulfillment can only thrive in HOLINESS. The treason of anxiety is that it has no CREATIVE POWER/IMPULSE. It lures its victim from the safehaven of HOPE and casts her into the delusion of "control"—a formidable doorless cellar. The victim shrivels in despair. Backed against a wall of frustration; she draws her knees up to support her bowed head and heart. Lifeless arms embrace the shell of a departed enthusiasm. The victim does not realize that she is the only living participant in this mirage.—HOPELESSNESS. She cannot die, because she has not lived. She does not LIVE because she is afraid to HOPE/PRAY. The natural realm for her is fear, pestilence, nausea and violence. To forfeit HOPE is to give oneSelf over to anxiety. Not even tears will attend this pathetic ceremony. Having begun in the SPIRIT, I can only prevail by the power of the Spirit.

The "breaking of the Yoke" of anxiety is SPIRIT work.

"that which is born of the flesh is flesh." (John 3:6) The flesh can only be Regenerated by the power of the HOLY SPIRIT. When I fully consent to the LOVE of GOD, I can HOPE again!

HOPE is the ambassador of the Kingdom.

HOPE is the life force of the Oblate.

HOPE is the conception and destiny of the Church.

> **Let us all RISE and Dance.**
> **Dance to the GLORY of GOD.**
> **Dance in the Joy of our HOPE.**
> **Dance in the Power of the unseen Kingdom.**
> **Dance with the poor.**
> **Dance in Amazement.**
> **Dance for the Healing of the NATIONS.**

COMMUNE WITH THINE HEART
and BE STILL

DEAR LORD,
    Teach me to be still when

COMMUNE WITH THINE HEART and BE STILL

SIX

"When you are disturbed, do not sin; ponder it on your beds, and be silent. Selah"

(Psalm 4:4)

Willful activity does not bring consolation of Soul. She responds only to the promptings of the Kingdom. The Soul is a vast potentiality of LIGHT, WISDOM, LOVE and PATHOS. One must fully consider Jesus, if one is to seriously ponder all the dimensions of Soul Life. To do so is to consent to being out of control and without a parachute! There is no rehearsal. God determines the hour and the circumstances. Like death, it is irreversible. JESUS, the open mystery. JESUS, the envelop of GRACE. JESUS, the homeless Messiah. JESUS, the authentic Sacrifice. Jesus the perpetual "Radiance of the Future." *(Jesus draw me into the power of this moment.)*

    A "project"/"program" entombed mind has much to overcome. "Stillness" is more a threat than a challenge. My will and abilities had become the unsolicited oppressors of my consciousness. To dislodge them meets with remarkable resistance. But SPIRIT prevails. I kiss them tenderly goodbye as a mother her children on the first day of school. Release from compulsion/control soothes the heart, relaxes the body; delights the senses. God can come to me now! GOD can express Divinity in my very bones. God can waste time watching me rest in Him. God can reveal to me the foliage of the Garden of Truth:
seen and unseen,
known and unknown,
alive and not born.
It's a picnic for the Soul. I am guest and beloved. Chosen and SILENT.

> From this MIDNIGHT in Eternity
> I shall give birth to mySELF.
> The velvety cloak that covers
> me is woven of the purple
> prayers of the intercessors.
> I am warmed. I am Blessed.
> I am Strengthened. I know
> that I am being prayed for.
> I can smell the incense. I
> feel HIS PRESENCE.

"Now at the time of the incense offering, the whole assembly of the people was praying outside."

(Luke 1:10)

SIX

This too is the Dance. Undistracted enfoldment, unveiling; quintessential BEING. Life in absolute motion. Experiencing breath, heartbeat release, PRESENCE. Silence is the Music.

In this praying the body knows every vowel—Language shapes itself. God hears. God speaks and the heart responds. My heart choreographs my desires; records each illumination; listens to the rhythms of my sorrow. The only true place of confidentiality—my Heart. Whether contrite or broken or bursting with Passion. To know me, God sees into my heart. LISTENS. And then God dances. A Slow Dance. A Lingering Dance. A supernatural motion of stillness. This stillness I have discovered results in an incredible.

Paradox: FIRE and SILENCE are united.

"Be still and know that I am God . . ." (Psalm 46:10)

How can there be PASSION in the Presence of the unknown?
What is there about *this* SILENCE that overwhelms
    while comforting?
Is this Pentecost FIRE, judgement fire, or both!?
Don't move! There's a FIRE.
The FIRE moves me; yet I am still.
Within me there is a hallowed burning. A deep combustion of PRAISE. A Dance has been conceived. God is breathing fire in me. God has torched my unbelief. Eternity is ablaze with JOY. PRAY to receive a spark from this Fire!
"BE STILL" until it comes.

A WORD ABOUT THE PASSION   SIX

The fire consumes me. An orgiastic splendor ignites my Soul. Every sensory engagement stimulates my anticipation. TOO MUCH for words. GROAN. WRITHE IN YOUR SOUL The TUMULT. THE THROBBING. An excessive consummation that bursts the seams of my imagined Resurrection. DRENCHED with excitement. Thrilled with the Mystery. I hear Mary asking "How can these things be, seeing I know not a man? if (Luke 1:34)

EMOTION is too incomplete.
Eroticism too bland. TOO mundane.
Reason too undeveloped.
This PASSION is of another sort.
God give me language!

I am completely thrown away in God.
Helpless.
Humiliated by everything ordinary.
Without Breath.
Needing to cry out.
There is no Sound.
The room is still.
The earth swoons.
God stands up.
The VISION is True.

It is emotion beyond feeling.
The body is active recipient and
     passive witness.
And yet I cannot MOVE.
Not even in thought.

STILLNESS has invaded my SOUL.

SIX

If you have ever walked knee-deep in a mystery, you understand. If you have ever seen the twilight of your own death, you understand. If you have ever experienced fear exorcised from your body, you really do understand. For you do not have to be taught how to be STILL. You Know. You already KNOW. The rest of us must learn stillness. Learn to *stop* ourselves:

> our thoughts—from controlling and resisting.
> our bodies—from movement.
> our mouths—from speaking.
> our pride—from justifying.

Pray for an inward STILLNESS. To do so is to *TRUST* GOD to think, to move, to speak, to defend! Pray to be still even in the Presence of adversity and disappointment. An inward STILLNESS that is totally given over to the GRACE of God. Your Body has been waiting for this DANCE. Your mind and your spirit also. Just to be still. This is a wonder. This is a song. "BE STILL," I say to my wandering mind. To my anxiety-ridden body and to all my insecurities. "BE STILL." And miraculously, I find mySelf breathing, again. What a life creating dance. I have begun to discover my body, my Soul and the power of breath! All our lives we live *in* our bodies. Yet for too long a time, our bodies remain unknown to us.

Only in this marvelous stillness do I come to know the movement of my breath, the beating of my heart, the heaving of my bosom, the "miracles" of sound and sight and touch. To run my tongue over my teeth and smile. To fondle my own neck. And to sit with myself. This is ecstasy. This is Peace.

I am getting to know my own body.

It is the mirror of my Soul.
It is a parable of my Soul.
It is the "magic" of GOD.

SIX

How can there be poetry in a body that is foreign to itself. No LIFE. No PASSION. It cannot float in waters. It cannot absorb the Sunlight. Too many nights needing God and unable to speak it. Too many journeys to distant lands with tears pouring out of my heart and eyes and no passenger to comfort me. Alone. Alone. With my SILENT GOD. Alone. Alone.

With the terror of my own mortality. To do good and regret it. To see the religious obstruct the forward movement of the Kingdom. To see evil applauded by the "righteous." This. Surely this is Hell! I will be still. I will not imperil my life further. I will send my soul away to a better place. "Vanity, vanity. All is vanity" (Ecclesiastes 1:2). I have forced my body to be awake, when she was desperate for sleep. To sit and sit and sit. When she wanted to run far, far away. To hold when she needed to let go. To stand, when compelled to fly. To make love when she desired most of all to be Alone. "Doing" has been the sin I have committed against myself. It has been my prescription for ignoring God. avoiding God. silencing God. controlling God. fighting God. punishing God. rejecting God. hurting God. banishing God. I will now choose "the better part."

> "Here I am LORD.
> Dry.
> Empty.
> Tired.
> a little frightened.
> Weary.
> Conflicted.
> Bored.
> Dispassionate.
> ANGRY.
> ALONE.
> ANXIOUS.
> MAD.
> MEAN.
> RESENTFUL.
> RESENTED.
> TIRED.
> Frustrated.
> Drowning in compulsion.

"But the Lord answered her, "Martha, Martha, you are worried and distracted by many things; there is need of only one thing. Mary has chosen the better part, which will not be taken away from her."

(Luke 10:41,42)

SIX

> Tempted.
> "Draw me nearer.
> Won't you?
> Draw me nearer."

This Dance is not without suspense, imagination or mystery. The Dancer must be still. My Body must give herself to the unknown. By the work of interior prayer and the contemplation of Eternity;

> anxiety
> distress
> frutration
> tension
> grief pass from me.

BREATH and BEAUTY—SPIRIT and HOPE are my complete reality. By these, I bless the world. Heal the Nations. Encourage my Soul. To "hurry" is to miss God. To "strive" is to cut off the life flow. Bells ring in this stillness to signal the approach of angels; the passage of a new generation; the creation of a rain drop. There is a cosmic pause, God is rousing the heavenlies. My SPIRIT rises straight up like a helicopter at take off. The ocean of finitude is beneath me. The sky of possibility surrounds me. The curtains of my emotion which had been drawn to shield me from the LIGHT are pulled open. I see the LOVE of God. I am free. I will lay before Him in adoration and thanksgiving.

> **"And when all the children of Israel saw how the fire came down, and the glory of the Lord upon the house, they bowed themselves with their faces to the ground upon the pavement, and worshipped, and praised the Lord, saying, For he is good; for his mercy endureth for ever."**
> **(2 Chronicles 7:3)**

This is the after Glow. The consumate PRESENCE. STILLNESS.

SIX

STILLNESS.
Rebel against the TO DO Culture.
"DOING" in the Name of God; but leaving Divinity behind.
STILLNESS.
Inward passivity.
Ambitionless.
Still.
To Be is to Breathe.
Slowly.
Fully.
Completely.
erotically.
compassionately.
freely.
ALIVE.
I shall not toy with distraction. Like an infant clinging to her mother's nipple once she has been fed.
To breathe is to pray.
Unhindered.
Unobstructed.
Immortality flowing.
This is a GIFT.
This IS Divine.
Sweet stillness.
I touch myself to discover if I am still here.
God touches me back just as a personal way of saying, "YES."

Dear CoJourner,

Take time to Breathe. To really Breathe. "Mary has chosen the better way." (Luke 10:41) Martha is lost in activity. LOST to herself. LOST from the PRESENCE of the LORD. Breath has gone out of her. LET US BREATHE Again. "BE STILL." "BE STILL." God Reigns. New patterns of PRAYER are born in Stillness. Fresh insight. Assurance and Great LIBERTY are the fruit of STILLNESS. IT'S TIME TO LIVE. GOD matters. STILLNESS is the first movement toward simplicity. "BE STILL" and learn how to pray.

SELAH

SIX

The "call to Emptiness" is a call to the "awareness" of the POWER of Breath.

BREATHE.
The Power of Release may be experienced in the act of BREATHE-ING.

BREATHE.
"Bad religion" has confounded our Spiritual Formation with excessive "doing."

BREATHE.
Allow God's Spirit to Guide us into a life of "BEING" HOLY.

BREATHE.
The aching in our souls is the accumulation
                        the build up
                        the excess of
rotting half truths and missed messages. We are sore from carrying the weight of poorly understood doctrines.
    We are weakened.
        Fatigued.
and Battered of Soul. We cannot BREATHE.

BE STILL and BREATHE.

BE STILL and RELEASE.

BE STILL and Be Aware.

Let your "ACTION" be in your BREATHE-ING.

When I take the time to BREATHE,
I open my life to the Health, PROSPERITY,
LOVE and BEAUTY that GOD has
deposited in the Universe for me
and for ALL. There is Abundance.
There is NO LACK. And so I
BREATHE.

COMMUNE WITH THINE HEART and BE STILL • 213

SIX

When I "choose" to be still, I am taking back the POWER over my life from "outside agents"—
> the committee
> the denomination
> the neighborhood
> the "guru"
> the "leader."

I will no longer be "agitated" by external forces. I "choose" to BREATHE. To know life. To become Universe aware. To Flow in Divinity. To BREATHE. This is Prayer.

It is part of the beautiful Romance of Prayer that in this season, the SPIRIT comes effortlessly. As I BREATHE, I am gentled to a STILL PLACE. Then it happens. I *am* BREATHED into an interior consciousness of GOD that supersedes any SPIRITUAL ENCOUNTER I have known. Only BREATHE.

> Passively.
> Humbly.
> Inwardly.

When The Soul reigns, the will collapses. Heaven opens. The universe yields. LIFE is saturated in a Glorious STILLNESS. BREATHE. And experience the life of GOD passing through your mortal BODY. BREATHE. And be warmed by the Reality of sacramental LOVE. This is prayer. This is PRAYER. The Soul is enthused by Heaven. Divinity skips through human circumstances. In the STILLNESS, I am healed of the wounds inflicted by delusion. In my STILL Place, I am LOST and FOUND in GOD. I BREATHE and I know.

GOD Breathes and I am known.
Be still and BE GOD's.

Complete the following Sentences:

I know it is time to BREATHE when

I will take back the power over my life from

WHEN I TAKE THE TIME TO BREATHE

SIX

"She had a sister named Mary, who sat at the Lord's feet and listened to what he was saying."

(Luke 10:39)

It is time to pray beyond the "awareness" of praying. It is time to pursue the opportunity to *really* know. To experience beyond experiencing. To plummet to the depths of intimacy with GOD. BREATHE. For only in STILLNESS can the Soul be taught to pray beyond knowing: Time. Mortality.
PAIN.
FEAR.
EROS.
HOPE.
GRIEF.
ANGER.
FATIGUE.
"God is Spirit." IN STILLNESS, SPIRIT PREVAILS and the Oblate comes to understand that the Realm of ultimate Belonging is Spiritual.

Fear of FACING GOD keeps the "religious" busy! A reluctance to test the borders of our mortality motivates unrelenting "distraction." Many lives are lived between Midnight and Morning. Many Visions disassembled. Many Supernatural rescue attempts declined.
If I could only "KEEP STILL."
  Beloved Cojourner,
  Look away from the "survival" issues of your existence. Take the power away from your personal suffering! BREATHE. And allow your awareness to rise to its highest plane—THE LOVE OF GOD. BE STILL. BREATHE. For your Soul's health. BREATHE. Allow your Body to be loved by the STILLNESS. LISTEN to the "Movement" of GOD. BREATHE. Experience the ascent-descent of supernatural prayer. Only BE STILL.

COMMUNE WITH THINE HEART and BE STILL • 215

PRAYER of The Soul LONGING TO HEAL ITSELF—   **SIX**
"Lord God of the unfathomable Depths of the Cosmos.
How shall I know you?
How can I surge beyond the clutter?
How can I consistently drink from Heavenly waters?
I am learning not to be afraid of my inner
    contradictions.
I am stepping out from under the canopy of shame.
Letting the LIGHT of your LOVE touch me directly.
Lord Jesus CHRIST.
Teach me to SEE LOVE.
    Trust LOVE.
    Receive LOVE.
    Give mySelf in LOVE.
I want to feel my body laughing.
Let it be so dear God.
Let this be my Reality.
Amen."

Having prayed such a prayer with all due confidence in the reality of GOD's Presence, LOVE, and faithfulness; BREATHE. Now is the time to set the book aside and lay before the LORD in STILLNESS. And when your time of closure arrives, simply PRAY THE LORD'S PRAYER.

SIX — WHEN THE SPIRIT OF DANCE RETURNS

Attempting to Dance again after so long a time; I feel clumsy, awkward, too fat, self conscious, embarrassed. But I am compelled.

The most meaningful prayer is the one I allow the SPIRIT to PRAY in me. "Come HOLY SPIRIT, COME." I will not circumvent your desire with my ego-ridden directives. I will not distort your voice with premature ejaculations. I will be STILL.

>Breathe.
>LISTEN.
>Release.
>"COME, Holy SPIRIT, COME."
>>How did I get so far away from myself?
>>One step at a time!
>>One day at a time!
>>One thought at a time.
>>Naively at first.

But then I became a psychological co-conspirator. I gave my mind to Sheol. And she gave me madness as my reward!

We have all heard it said that "STILL WATERS run deep." And so it is. Quite often, when we become still, it gives an opportunity for unreconciled turbulence to rise from deep places in our lives. This is not the time to panic, flee or be intimidated. But from the vantage of our <u>STRONG</u>, STILL PLACE in the LORD we can discern the chaos, SPEAK THE NAME of JESUS to it and learn the lesson it holds for our life.

Then BREATHE.

>STILLNESS teaches many personal lessons. LESSONS once learned, LIBERATE and EMPOWER.
>Illumine and HEAL.

TESTIMONY:

>I struggled over a long period of time to practice "STILLNESS" as a Spiritual Discipline. Having identified a recurring battle between emotion and FAITH, I determined to seek the path of Integrity. To allow myself to peek beneath my feelings. To attempt to sort out what creates the intensity of my responses. TO LISTEN. TO LISTEN. To defuse Pride. I began to slowly look at the moment, to consider my life. TO LISTEN.

COMMUNE WITH THINE HEART and BE STILL • 217

Suddenly I realized that when I am disappointed with mySelf, I make my complaint against the Lord:

> **"Will you be angry with us forever? Will you prolong your anger to all generations?" (Psalm 85:5)**

When I wake up to myself, I give expression to my deep sorrow. A sponge has soaked up all my JOY. I am dry and brittle on the inside. I need to PRAY or I will die. God help me to PRAY. God move the lips of my SOUL and help me to PRAY. GOD burst the seams of this bondage and PLEASE help me to pray. I forgive EVERYONE but the devil himself. God help me PRAY! Are you so FAR from my longing? So indifferent to my emptiness? PRAY God! Until there is laughter in my SOUL again. Again. AGAIN. "My friends" could not GO the distance. Only YOU and I are out on this ROCK. Let living waters flow out of ME God. Effortlessly. FREELY. Absolutely. Amen.

> *"LORD have Mercy upon me*
> *before this present madness*
> *takes hold.*
> > *In the Name of Jesus I pray"*
> > > *Amen.*

To be still in the Presence of GOD is to be "safe." Urgencies, crises, emergencies lose their "charm." The "spell" of action is broken! To speak the Name of Jesus is to pray completely. It is to arrest every distracting motion. It is to reconcile the conflict of desire and obedience. "JESUS." It is to be raised to supernatural awareness.
When I become STILL, prayer finds me, enfolds me, cultivates my Soul.
I am STILL.
My Soul is STILL.
I can BREATHE.

SIX

COMPELLED TO PREVAIL IN PRAYER

"And the LORD continued, "See, there is a place by me where you shall stand on the rock;"

(Exodus 33:21)

SIX

"STILL WATERS RUN DEEP." To "be still" is an act of courage. It is a willingness to face GOD and OneSelf. Whatever rises, the Holy Spirit is *READY* to receive. Issues that are too painful or disorienting should be prayerfully shared with a mental health professional. THIS TOO IS COURAGE!

"Holy Spirit of GOD
shape my LIFE in this STILLNESS.
Breathe in me THE ARDOR of YOUR LOVE.
Flood my Soul with the mysteries
*   of the Kingdom.*
BREATHE in ME THE ARDOR of YOUR WORD.
Touch my LIFE with the INNER CHARM
*   of simplicity.*
BREATHE in ME THE ARDOR of YOUR NAME.

Holy SPIRIT, Blessed Holy SPIRIT
Dispel the shadows of guilt and shame
*   and fear.*
Holy SPIRIT, ALL POWERFUL Holy SPIRIT
Commune with my heart that you are
*   ever near.*

I can be STILL HOLY SPIRIT
because you are
with me,
within me, and
you LOVE Me."
*   Amen.*

Now BREATHE.
BE STILL.
BREATHE.
And let the
PRAYER
fill you.

COMMUNE WITH THINE HEART and BE STILL

I have recognized for some time now that PRAYING/DANCING in or near the waters brings almost immediate REFRESHMENT. Calm. Serenity. For others it is the Sun, A Garden, a Window. But for me the WATERS are my Altar of Perpetual RESTORATION. The sand beneath my feet, the darkened sky, the liquid hush that circles my ankles, my calves, my thighs. I speak to Heaven. I am embraced by angels. GOD is NOT DEAD. Forever rests upon my heart. I lift my arms in PRAISE. The stars begin to dance. God sways with the waters. I respond in song:

> "Draw me Nearer
> Nearer Blessed Lord
> to Thy precious bleeding side."
> (A.M.E. Hymnal, Hymn 283)

My body becomes one with the WATERS. ONE WITH GOD. ONE IN SONG. ONE in PRAYER. We are ONE. The Dance is ALIVE. Healing. Blessing. Liberating. Revelation is at hand. I will see. I will hear. I will know. This body now becomes a channel of Eternity. The RIVERS flow through me: TRUTH, MERCY, REDEMPTION, BLESSING and PEACE. I will never be ashamed Again!

The ministry of Creation is to direct us to that STILL place that is within each of us. To mirror for us the power of simplicity and the permanence of Beauty. The human being devoid of STILLNESS has no compass, sense of place or direction. When we are STILL, we sit closest to GOD. There is perfect communion that can only be discovered in STILLNESS. A purity of innocence. A depth of intimacy. A healing of all separations. We no longer experience our bodies as weapons but rather as channel's of Divinity.

SIX

"For you have delivered my soul from death, and my feet from falling, so that I may walk before God in the light of life."

(Psalms 56:13)

SIX

"O LORD God of hosts, hear my prayer; give ear, O God of Jacob! Selah"

(Psalms 84:8)

"Lord Jesus Christ,
Son of the LIVING God—
"Draw me nearer"
Let me feel the Pulse
of your GRACE.
"Draw me nearer"
Let me drink from
the waters of your tears.
"Draw me nearer"
Help me find a hiding place
in your wounded side.
"Draw me nearer"
Behold my agony and
have MERCY upon me.
"DRAW me nearer"
and heal me of the sins
that have been committed against my body.
"DRAW me nearer"
And breathe LIFE into
my failing HOPE.
"Draw me Nearer"
Take me out of reach
of the clutches of depression.
"DRAW me Nearer"
by your LOVE, your Blood,
Your NAME—
    JESUS,
    JESUS,
    JESUS.
"DRAW ME NEARER."
To that STILL place
in your LOVE
where fear can never
touch me again.
              AMEN.

It is time now to bring the REALITY of my Soul life out of the foreign terrain of dependence and into the realm of personal responsibility.

It really is time now to erase the compulsions of "religious" behaviors and pursue an authentic Christ consciousness. I have walked into the last brick wall of the denominational reward and punishment system and the only option is to fly over it. This too is a good thing!

Sitting here. It's Saturday. In the Rain. I have an intriguing sense of freedom and HOPE. Lately, I no longer feel bound. I have been released from the former things—anxiety, fear, unforgiveness, intimidation, infirmity and desperation. God told me that my angel Zohar (Radiance, Splendor, Light) is with me and I am Knowing it NOW!

I know it in my thought realm as an incredible energy—force of mind surges through my consciousness.

I know it in my body as a sense of REST, tranquility and Assurance render me WELL, WHOLE, CENTERED.

I know it in my Spirit as supernatural horizons impinge on my historical predicament giving me SIGHT and INSIGHT.

Today FOREVER has come to me.

"Watch with me and PRAY" (Matthew 26:28)—why don't you?
The God world of sanctification is an odyssey of sorts. (I don't know why Spirit chose this word "odyssey"). I have finally, perhaps reached the point where I am no longer in danger of exploiting myself!

INTERESTING.

Only GOD can love me when I am STILL.
Only GOD respects the dignity of this Holy space. Only GOD will offer me music to accompany the movement of my heart.
Because GOD embraces every STILL moment with Eternity.

> **TO THE COJOURNER—**
> *Take off your shoes, your attitude, your robes of identity, when you enter your still place. When you return to the world, do not be amazed to find that you no longer "need" them. SELAH.*

SIX

"These Jews were more receptive than those in Thessalonica, for they welcomed the message very eagerly and examined the scriptures every day to see whether these things were so."

(Acts 17:11)

SIX

I am born to SPEAK, to DREAM, to WORD, to WAIT. To DANCE.
I am born the Woman who HEARS the grieving of the unborn. Who dies a thousand midnights before morning. Who hears the rattling of the skeletal frame swallowed up in an immensity of flesh. Who watches helplessly as the reluctant church nauseates itself denying JESUS. Who watches her first love die and then her second and loses her memory.
Who sees insanity held out before her as a stretcher of rescue.
Nevertheless, to me has been GIFTED the VISION—
"Thy Kingdom Come."
Woman, Woman, Africa Woman, Diaspora Daughter,
Did you drink the CUP OF SORROW?
Did you sip the wine while it was still
                water?
                Unchanged.
                clear.
                impotent.
Have you been given the "new wine?"
    or the "sponge sopped in vinegar?"
                                      (Mark 15:36)
Stop running and drink.
Be still and drink.
Breathe deeply
and DRINK.
Slowly.
Drink.
The nations await your rising.
The Cathedral bell is silent.
Its doors thrown ajar.
Drummers line the walkway.
The procession awaits your rising.
Be STILL and listen.
Be STILL.
LISTEN.
Give GOD your body.
GIVE.
Let GENEROSITY be unhindered.
BREATHE.

COMMUNE WITH THINE HEART and BE STILL

SIX

Let your heart flow toward Heaven.
Allow streams of Glory to be poured into your empty places.
WAIT.
REST.
BREATHE.
BE STILL.
    My heart knows who God is.
    My heart listens for the footsteps of the LORD
and then races to welcome Him. BEAMING with JOY.
The heart can out run fatigue.
The heart can Silence unbelief with a glance.
The heart can Heal the mind.
(The reverse is not true.)
So let prayer be a matter of the heart.
The heart lives Eternal.
Eternal unto the LORD.
When I am still; my Heart RESTS.
Draws in Light.
Increases in strength.
Blesses my Body.
Listens to the Wind.
PRAYS.
Forever comes near.
Today is a Song.
CHRIST is RISEN.
CHRIST is RISEN.
CHRIST is Alive and Risen.
ALIVE in me.
STILL in me.
STILL with me.
STILL.
    SELAH.

SIX

Stillness is not the hand maiden of the recluse. It is the furnace of the Warrior Queen. In stillness, she is made ready for her Destiny. In STILLNESS, the Apocalypse of HOPE pours down VISIONS of Restoration upon her Soul. She Knows that to BE STILL is to consent to a Supernatural alignment with Holy Trinity—GOD.

She emerges from the furnace as an INFERNO. This FIRE cannot be quenched!

She is THE STILL FIRE that awaits the command of GOD.

The men fear "reputation."
    "JOB Security."
        "upward mobility."
        "natural" power.
This woman FEARs GOD!

SHE IS STILL.
Her Soul is a burning fountain.
She WAITS ONLY FOR GOD.

(You will need an invitation to come to this DANCE!)

When GOD says so, her LIFE becomes Ablaze with prophecy. You can **read** her Prayer in the movement of her Body. You can **experience** the force by the glow upon her COUNTENANCE. GOD has been preparing her. The heavens stand STILL in anticipation. The tide cannot be turned back. She is the **ONE**.

    Resolute as Vashti.
    Wild as Hagar.
    Courageous as Rahab.
    Descendent of Nzinga.

    Only GOD would "choose" her. Only GOD.
    The NATIONS do not esteem her.
    The Church does not regard her.
    The men do not "see" her.
    The women do not "approve" of her.

COMMUNE WITH THINE HEART and BE STILL

SIX

Only GOD understands her.
    NEEDS her.
    WAITS FOR her.
       Selah.
She has learned that to BE STILL is to be Alone with GOD.
Alone with the VISION.
Alone in Eternity.
To be STILL is to HOPE alone.

What she once feared; she now Embraces. She can BREATHE. She flows in Divinity. The nations have been placed in her bosom to drink of TRUTH. Through her they must learn to be STILL from idle controversies. They shall become CHRIST aware. GOD Knows.
                ONLY GOD Knows.

For while the VISION is for the NATIONS; her heart continues to cry out to the LORD for Africa; dear Africa. "When you pray, won't you please say, 'AFRICA'?" Let our lives be a perpetual intercession unto the LORD from generation to generation. With our praying let us Create a New Future in GOD—unknown.
           un-named.
           un-Defiled.

       "Nkosi Sikelel'i—Afrika"
        (GOD BLESS AFRICA)

Suffering humanity.
We have had our body WONDER exploited.
    our strength stolen.
    our creativity squandered.
    our Health dissipated.
    our resources plundered.
    our children traumatized.
    our HOPE crushed.
    our dignity ridiculed.
    our lives impaled.
    our heritage marketed.
    our Forgiveness betrayed.

SIX

*"Give a thought to
 Africa,
'Neath the burning
 sun.
There are hosts of
 weary hearts
 waiting to be won.
Many lives have passed
 away;
On swamps and sod.
There are voices
 crying now.
For the living God.*

*Tell the LOVE
  of JESUS.
  By the Hills and
   Waters.
God Bless Africa
  AND her sons
  and
  daughters"*

(A.M.E. Hymnal 564)

"Woza Moya Woza"
(Come Holy SPIRIT Come)

Grieving humanity.
We have buried our dead while their dreams were still living.
        brooding.
        creating.
        speaking.
        liberating.

"Udumo Lwayo"
(Hear our Prayers)

Anointed Humanity.
We have the consent of the Almighty to lay hold of our DESTINY.
To arouse the women to RISE before dawn and conspire with GOD.

(PRAY IT OVER and
    Over and
        OVER again.)

Pray IT until African and Diasporic peoples manifest the GLORY of GOD in the midst of the nations.

"GOD BLESS AFRICA
and her sons
    and daughters!"

It is the RESURRECTION that creates the balance between the unformed future and my present HOPE. Daily I cry to "Abba" in hidden places where no terror can find me. Joyless hymns crack the walls of sanctuaries where no children sing. They are dead. Having died in the mosaic of adult pretensions. But, "the prayers of the saints availeth much." Let us take the excursion to ecstasy. A beauteous treasure lines the corridors of our prayer life. PEACE, it seems, is achievable! The mantle of the PEACEMAKER is a heavenly light. Her countenance. Her touch. Her lips. Her song. Her courage.
She is the LIGHT bringer.
She is Abba's daughter.
She dances before the LION of Judah.
"Take courage, O my Soul."
"Some day" is coming soon.
"Some day" has risen in our hearts.
"Some day" awaits us on the banks of the Nile.
All is FORGIVEN.
All is well.

I shall await my SILENCE now.
The wordless Wonder of His Presence.
The mist of Revelation from His thoughts.
The music of His footsteps.
The Silent LIGHT.
The Beautiful STILLNESS.

This is a breath away from Rapture. A glimpse of the "new earth." The one where each of our little ones has a childhood. The one where the Son of God is not legislated out of the culture. The one where African women bead the hair of their virgin daughters, baptize their sons into the mystery and anoint their husbands with eucalyptus oil.

In STILLNESS, harmony is not spelled uniformity. And gender does not become idolatry. To be STILL is to wait with GOD. Self knowledge comes to the one who does not reject STILLNESS. Only when I am STILL can I see the patterns of my lives.

BEHOLD THE WOMAN.

SIX

"Therefore confess your sins to one another, and pray for one another, so that you may be healed. The prayer of the righteous is powerful and effective."

(James 5:16)

SIX

"so shall my word be that goes out from my mouth; it shall not return to me empty, but it shall accomplish that which I purpose, and succeed in the thing for which I sent it."

(Isaiah 55:11)

The future has come upon me.
TODAY, I perceive Abba weaving of the threads of my life a GARMENT of Hope for the Nations.

TODAY, I celebrate Deliverance from Fear,
Death and Powerlessness.

TODAY, "I roll my works upon the WORD
of the LORD and they are accomplished!" (Proverbs 16:3)

TODAY, I know Myself as the Daughter of
the Church, the Apostle of Hope.

TODAY, I experience MySelf as
the Dance Bringer.

TODAY, I receive the LIGHT.

TODAY, I am kept in the
STILLNESS of GOD.

Dear Cojourner
   "DESIGN" A Today for
   yourself that opens your heart,
   brings forth laughter,
   celebrates generosity AND
   LISTENS to the STILLNESS
   of GOD.

COMMUNE WITH THINE HEART and BE STILL • 229

I recognize the POWER alive within me. I sense the Unchanged MOOD of God concerning me. Compulsion and striving are beginning to diminish. Health means consenting to one's own Purpose. It is the *natural* result of Spiritual Harmony. The LOSS of inward stillness creates disease of Soul and Body. Be still and catch up with GOD.

Our GOD Who Is.
> Is Light.
> Is Power.
> Is Beauty.
> Is LOVE.
> Is Truth.
> Is Redemption.
> Is Health.

In stillness, I permit my very breath to become Prayer.
> *Jesus Christ, Son of the Living God.*
> *Jesus Christ, Son of the Living God.*
> *Jesus Christ, Son of the Living God.*

Breath dances through my BEING until I am ONE with God.
> In this praying my body responds to the language of God. Every vowel is known. God speaks and my heart responds. God speaks and there is fluttering in my soul. Because my lips stammer, my heart choreographs my desires. Each illumination is recorded. God dances to the rhythms of my sorrow. I have discovered that my heart is the only TRUE place of confidentiality. Whether filled with contrition or bursting with Passion, my heart does not betray me. To know me, God peers into my heart. LISTENS. WEEPS. And then God dances. A slow dance. A

SIX

SIX

lingering dance. A Supernatural MOTION in Stillness. This is the paradox of ecstasy! In this uniquely Supernatural moment, there is an incredible *sensory* Awakening. I begin to really experience mySelf. Whole consciousness is ignited—

>Color
>Sound
>delight
>Pain/Agony
>VISION/vision
>shadow
>Presence—
>the elements: earth, wind, fire, water

I am more fully present to LIFE as a sensate Reality. A LIVING being. I am Alive. A Prima Dona in the whole Cosmic Dance. Pulsating with Supernatural capabilities. Aflame with the Signature of God. WRITHING with JOY. My very body is speaking in tongues. The Self is wasting away in God. The Soul incarnates as Person. And not, a Sound to be heard in the natural realm. Nothing astir! There is motion beyond seeming. God is inspired. I am undistracted. No longer attempting to reason with the dEvil, I lay beside the "still waters."

>(Psalm 23:2)

In the stillness, the Prayers of the intercessors cover me with a velvety cloak. From this MIDNIGHT, I ascend to the VISION of Eternity. I know that I am being prayed for. I smell the incense. I feel God's Presence.

The angel of the LORD, my angel, Zohar defends me.
PERSONAL PRAYER guides me as I draw in LIGHT, BREATH, ONENESS, WONDER and GENEROSITY.
The thoughts of the dancer.
The faculties of the dancer.
The soul of the dancer
  are consumed by the PASSION of the Dance.

SIX

It is 11:36 p.m. on a friday. I know this. "Lord Jesus Christ Son of the LIVING GOD, Have Mercy upon Me." The Prayer of the Pilgrim rests well with me. I can feel the organs in my body clamoring for perfection. God is happening to me. Right NOW.
"You are a garden locked up, my sister, my bride; you are a spring enclosed, a sealed fountain."
     (Song of Solomon 4:12)
The LOVE of my Bridegroom is Healing me.
My body responds with Joy and innocence.
This is sacred awakening.
My feet are bare.
My head is bare.
My soul is Naked and unashamed.
There is an orchid on the Altar. Placed there just for me. I have come to join my Beloved.
She who would dance with God.
Must first learn to be still with God.
  Close.
  Dear.
  At Peace.
This Rhapsody is For the Nations!
I will plunge the Supernatural Depths of Critical Consciousness.
I am the interrogative and the exclamation!
There is breadth in Vision.
Not as austere as the "Articles" of One's Religion.
Rather bouyant
 and fluid
 and formless without being chaotic.
The Spirit of Dance/Prayer has returned to me.
I receive it in the Name of Jesus. Amen.

SIX

"Be still, and know that I am God! I am exalted among the nations, I am exalted in the earth."

(Psalms 46:10)

I renounce the distractions of my Soul Life. The waters have been parted for me. Oh the minutes, the hours, the days, the weeks, the years given over to infirmity and depression. I had never been taught the discipline of Stillness. The "to do" culture is so debilitating. The over-againstness so severe. Racism so comprehensive. The only deterrent to madness and disease is Personal Prayer. It is strenuous and rigorous. Being in solidarity with every JUST and RIGHTEOUS Cause is overwhelming; to say the least! To Dance for the PEACE of the Nations renders the heart weary. STILLNESS is not given, it must be seized! I must part the waters of the Cosmos and Enter. I must blazon a path through the clutter of Reality and ENTER. For there is Always, always activity in the Supernatural Realm. Every moment is infused with the call and response of SPIRIT and Nature. But only Still draws the LIGHT.

        orders my thoughts.
        centers my perspective.
        opens my world!

STILL permits the HOLY SPIRIT to commune with my Soul. My gift is an undistracted consciousness. I have the Power to consent or decline this Dance. I covenant to believe in BEAUTY, DIGNITY, PURPOSE. I set myself within range of the Eternal by releasing myself fully to the Mind of God.

STILL.
SILENT.
AWARE.
OPEN.

I shall conceive the DANCE
        for the New Day.
        for the New Generation.
        for the New World.

This is the will of the Kingdom of Heaven.

Dear Cojourner,   **SIX**

It is my JOY to make an offering of PRAYERS that bring stillness to the heart. PRAYERS that shape our Soul life in stillness. PRAYERS that water the seeds of stillness in the garden of our Reality. These 7 prayers are mere beginnings. GATES of Departure. Only the HOLY SPIRIT knows the depths to which GOD will take us at any particular MOMENT. Every Oblate yearns for that "Secret Place" of the MOST HIGH (Psalm 91). Nevertheless, we must "BE STILL" if we are to ENTER.

PRAY FOR:
- INTENTION—when you sense you are not fully living in God's will.
- INTEGRITY—when you have done violence to another's spirit, or to the covenant, or to the Church.
- PURIFICATION—when you recognize that you walk in unrighteous desire, preoccupation or covetousness.
- HEALING—when physical or emotional disease is your reality.
- ENDUEMENT—when you are willing for GOD to use you for others.
- RADIANCE—when you are ready to LIVE ONLY for GOD.
- RESTORATION—when you are willing to do SPIRITUAL WARFARE for Africa, The DIASPORA, and the nations.

These are PRAYERS that call us to DEEPER dimensions of Spirituality. PRAYERS that teach us how to breathe again.
Don't Rush.
Follow the Holy Spirit.
Remain in the Flow.
BREATHE in the STILLNESS of GOD.

"Breathe IN the Stillness of GOD"

SIX

Dear Cojourner,

In these 7 prayers,

Center the activity in the rhythmn of your breathing.

PROSTRATE YOURSELF.
Allow stillness to flow from the TOP of your head to the soles of your feet.

Experience Breath become Prayer become breath. In STILLNESS.

**BECOME ONE PRAYER,
ONE BREATH,
ONE REALITY,
WITH GOD**

PRAYER of INTENTION:

Mind of Christ
ingenious,
perfect,
bosom of TRUTH—
possess my thoughts
Reign in my faculties.
Illumine.
Ignite.
Transform.   AMEN

"Breathe IN the Stillness of GOD"

"Breathe IN the Stillness of GOD" **SIX**

PRAYER OF INTEGRITY:

SPIRIT of Christ.
Holy ONE.
Eternal.
Sovereign.
Enter NOW my fractured will.
Repair.
Cleanse.
Shape.
Direct.
AMEN.

"Breathe IN the Stillness of GOD"

SIX

"I am weary with my moaning; every night I flood my bed with tears; I drench my couch with my weeping."

(Psalms 6:6)

PRAYER OF PURIFICATION:

Blessed Jesus,
    even NOW.
    even NOW.
    even NOW.
Produce in my very Body
cells of regeneration.
cells of Holiness.
WRITE your Name upon my Soul.
    Diminish every tendency of Rebellion
    Purge me with the FIRES of conviction.
    Amen.

"Breathe IN the Stillness of GOD"   **SIX**

PRAYER OF HEALING:

Life,
Death and
Resurrection
of JESUS CHRIST
flow in my
    Circulatory System
    Respiratory System
    Digestive System
    Nervous System
LET Your RADIANCE NOW
permeate my Immune System
with Healing Life.
Flow throughout my memories
    HOLY SPIRIT
Remove every diseased cell
    of flesh
    personality
    spirit.
    Amen.

"Breathe IN the Stillness of GOD"

SIX

"Blessed be the God and Father of our Lord Jesus Christ! By his great mercy he has given us a new birth into a living hope through the resurrection of Jesus Christ from the dead,"

(1 Peter 1:3)

"Breathe IN the Stillness of GOD"

PRAYER OF ENDUEMENT:

Holy Jesus
as I remain
before you.
Yielded.
Believing.
Praying.
BAPTIZE me
with the Dance of Holiness.
That when YOU Dance
with me,
I shall
"lay hands on the sick and
they shall be Healed" (Mark 16:18)

demons shall flee from
the Sanctity of Your
Presence.

Kings shall repent.

The poor will be made rich.

The wealthy will turn to you.

O God,
Messiah.
My thoughts
imagination,
memory,
belong to you.
      Amen

"Breathe IN the Stillness of GOD"

"Breathe IN the Stillness of GOD"   **SIX**

PRAYER OF RADIANCE:

Glorious JESUS,
Beautify me with Your Light.
Perfect me with your *gaze*.
I want to be a reflection of your Glory.
Illumine my Heart.
Shine upon my Imagination.
Flood my Soul with Perpetual songs
to your GLORY.
           Amen.

"Breathe IN the Stillness of GOD"

SIX

"Breathe IN the Stillness of GOD"

PRAYER OF RESTORATION:

Son of God; I want to be Your Bride.
I want to be Your Covenant Beauty.
Confer upon me your forgiveness.
Do not send me away,
my Abba,
my Jewel,
my Song.
Heal and Restore my Africa and Diaspora.
Peel from our lives the layers of violence and shame.
Cause us to REPOSSESS the wealth
                        DIGNITY
                        Land and
                        HOPE
that injustice
evil and
disobedience to your LIGHT have
    stolen from us.
LOOK upon us AGAIN
    with favor
        through GRACE.
LORD I stand in the GAP
    for my Africa and DIASPORA.
    LORD Have MERCY.
    LORD FORGIVE.
    LORD Have MERCY.
I speak the Name
of Jesus
to escort these
confessions
petitions and
intercessions
    to Your Throne.
                AMEN.

"Breathe IN the Stillness of GOD"

THE DANCE COMES.
And although it is mine to "wait,"
I know that I shall be taken over.
I welcome her.
I welcome her.
There is a sort of artistic disorder in my uncreated space.
It is tintillating, inspiring.
If I let myself GO;
I will fly.
I will really Fly.
    This is how I wait for God.
One breath at a time.
One breath at a time.
One breath at a time.
STILL.
Utterly Still.

Within each of us is the desire and the capacity for stillness. It is a "gift." A sacred gift.
Unacknowledged.
Unclaimed.
Unprotected.
But it has been given to us.

SEEK IT.
DISCOVER ITS Beauty.
Experience the POWER of IT.
LIVE the LESSONS Learned from it.
SIMPLY—
    "BE STILL."
And in the fullness of TIME.
The Dance will be Born in you.
Gently.
Quietly.
Completely.
Passionately.
You will experience Your Soul begin
Dancing within you.

SIX

"From ages past no one has heard, no ear has perceived, no eye has seen any God besides you, who works for those who wait for him."

(Isaiah 64:4)

"he made the storm be still, and the waves of the sea were hushed."

(Psalms 107:29)

SIX

Dear Cojourner,
    Consider the lessons this DANCE has taught you.
    What vow will you make to the LORD? What Covenant of LOVE? What witness in the World? What kindness to your body?
        LIFE IS A GIFT.
        LIFE REALLY IS.
    My Prayer to GOD for us all, as we prepare to close, is that this Dance will flood the world with waters of generosity. That this mystery—PRAYER—will raise up daughters of Oblation,
        enthuse the Church and
        reoncile the NATIONS.
    I am praying that you will join me in praying that for every racist or pornographic or anti-Christian book that is sold; a copy of this book will also be purchased; in the NAME of JESUS.
    I am praying that the SPIRIT of DANCE will fire WONDER in the hearts of Women every where.
    I am praying that this DANCE will live forever. . .
    I am praying that morning Sun and midnight thunder will behold the Dance in you.
    I am praying that your Healing will rise the very moment you trust your self to Dance.
    I am praying that the vocabulary of our prayer lives will include STILLNESS and
SILENCE and
TRANSITION.
    I am praying that these prayings will be taught to the children of every generation from henceforth.
    In the Name of
        JESUS.
            AMEN.

THE GLORY and the DANCE and the GLORY

I DANCE with GOD because

THE GLORY and the DANCE and the GLORY

SEVEN

> "For Thine is the Kingdom,
> and the POWER,
> and the GLORY,
> FOREVER."

To have been "found" by GOD in the garden of our unknowing is an awesome thing!
Having gazed at life through the eyes of fear and then suddenly to have the scales removed along with every sense of limitation is a supernatural moment!

Like "Blind Bartemeus," I now see! I see the lights in the city of my experience. The side streets and alley ways no longer create dread. The skyline of my potentialities depicts an extraordinary architectural flair. And hidden throughout are innumerable sanctuaries—a kiss, a florist shop, a whiff of tea rose, the sound of Kathleen Battle in the morning, not to mention, the endless sky. Like a young eagle wounded in flight, I will get my bearing/my healing and fly again. So many have died before seeing their own beauty/worth/DIGNITY.
They died before giving birth to themselves.
They died before experiencing authentic reality—
> self awareness
> self knowledge
> self affirmation.

When Death comes before FREEDOM, this is the ultimate indignity. There is no crime more heinous. Because NOTHING does greater violence to the Cosmic Soul. For the Oblate, the whole adventure of life is the SEEKING after SIGHT.
The pursuit of Vision.
The desperate grasping for LIGHT.
The deep longing for illumination.
To live, to SEE.
To see the core of one's life meaning.
To see the connectedness of the Universe to a solitary life.
To see the wings of summer in one ray of Sunlight on a December morning.
To see the tears of GOD as one endures personal suffering.

"The blind man said, 'Rabbi I want to see.' Jesus said, "your Faith has healed you.' Immediately he received his sight..."

(Mark 10:51,52)

SEVEN

At last, when the Oblate is able to say with assurance—
"I have seen the Vision of GOD for the Nations!" or
"I see the balcony of the Eternal!" or
"I see my life work."
To do so, is to make peace with life. Not to do so, is to be forever striving against the wind. "I once was blind, but NOW I SEE." (A.M.E. Hymnal #226)

    Dear Cojouner,
    Pray to SEE.
    To see the Universe open at your very coming.
    To see the Souls of your "enemies."
    To see the power of simplicity.
    To see the moving force within a STILL Truth.
    To see Goodness.
    To see winged angels dancing.
    PRAY to SEE.

The invisible chords of Eternity uniting us with every people in every generation.
    The Silence that comes at the end of warfare and destruction.
    The hearts of humanity conquered by LOVE.

    PRAY TO SEE JESUS—
    Opening the gates of the City.
    Tearing down the strongholds of corruption.
    Baptizing the children.
    Embracing the men.
    Sharing mysteries with the women.
    Anointing you with oil.
    Anointing You with oil.
    Anointing You with oil.

    SELAH.

The LORDship of Jesus Christ is an ascending reality as faith bursts the ceilings of knowledge and experience. I see JESUS even before the dawn has come. I see JESUS enrobed in glorious splendor walking on the mist of morning pronouncing benedictions upon the earth.

THE GLORY AND THE DANCE AND THE GLORY

SEVEN

The light of a million thousand sunrises form a halo around HIS head. The gold from all the mines on the earth and all the diamonds line the hem of his garment. The stars of every midnight sky circle round the body of His Purple velvet robe. The shimmering pink glow of Heaven opening frames this apocalypse. And God walks on a path of peridot stones that lead from Glory to glory to GLORY.

As I lower my eyes and back, I stretch toward the Son and he touches my life with His LIGHT and I am RADIANT.

I extend my arms like eagle's wings as my body prepares to leap from the cliff of doubt into the promise of the heavenlies. God raises my feet to the sky. I am soaring in my Soul.

My body is resistance-free.
    fear-free.
    anxiety-free.
    Un-"controlled."
There is breath.
Spirit is breath.
Spirit is life.
I am the Wind.
All is well within.
All is well with my Soul.
The forces of gravity—
                financial, relationship and denominational issues no longer have the POWER to bring me DOWN.

For some weeks now I had barely walked the earth. A remarkable silence had blanketed my life.
I had found my Quiet ZONE.
I was in harmony with all the LOVE in the Universe.
I experienced "perfect" balance for the first TIME,
        "GODLINESS with CONTENTMENT
                is GREAT GAIN."
                          (I Timothy 6:6)

SEVEN

Reflect on this dear Cojouner.
Through what doors do we pass to enter the regions of our discontent?
How do we shut them forever?
"CONTENTMENT" is a remarkable emotion. Too often wrongly associated with nursing babies and the aged. To be found by GOD in the garden of my unknowing was to be gently taken over by the POWER of CONTENTMENT.
No delight.
No thunder.
No expectation. As I was being expressed in passages of unrelenting transformation, I had but one desire.
    I must know GOD.
    I must fully manifest this Holy Light that I see in my heart. And yes,
    I am learning that STILLNESS *precedes* illumination.
GOD has become REALITY.
    Total REALITY.
    Prevailing REALITY.

I have stepped out of all defenses; my soul now lingers by the waters of transfiguration. I seek immersion in the light of GOD—inward and outward. Change is a profound matter of consent; of will; of intention. GOD knows. God stands on the horizon where the waters are deepest and beckons me out of my shadow and into the RADIANCE. Calling me. Calling me. Calling me to the LIGHT. The very sound of LOVE melts the stiffness in my body. Silences rigidity. Unleashes enthusiasm. I FEEL the laughter of GOD. I feel the Divinity in the universe. I feel the POWER of my becoming. I have stepped into Holy water!

THE GLORY AND THE DANCE AND THE GLORY • 247

SEVEN

I am washed!
The pure Love of GOD is my motivation.
A pure Desire for GOD shapes my Life.
Vanity perishes.
I see trees now.
    the skyline.
    blades of grass in winter.
I see Hope.
    Desire.
    Passion.
    Innocence.
    Beauty.
I see the womb of GOD. And I am in it.

    Each of us having received the bread and the wine; waited at the empty tomb;
and stood within the walls of Pentecost becomes a "light to the nations." Satan lurches at us in a last ditch attempt to dissuade us from the shores of RADIANCE. It is too late. Our feet are already wet! No mirage or memory can change our course of action. The healing in the waters ignites an undaunted Faith. GOD REIGNS.

        "I am persuaded that
        neither height nor depth
        nor things present nor
            things to come
        can separate me from
        the LOVE of God which
        is in Christ Jesus. (Romans 8:35)

    At last! This is the assurance that every woman lives for—that she is unconditionally LOVED! Who can refuse to Dance upon hearing such a proclamation. Even when I know that to Dance is to be changed forever.
    Every Cojourner "needs" to Dance.
To experience immortality.
To release her limitations.
To "own" her Divinity.
To be shaped by this moving intimacy.
To love her own body!
To ride the wings of Prayer.

SEVEN

To disengage her JOY from the delusion of "success."
To REST.
To Heal.
To see the Morning star rise!

The human body can be set free from mortal captivity, cultural exploitation and personal rejection. This body knows the secrets of Divinity. This Body is the living space of GOD. This Body has incarnated Eternity.

The healer can be healed!

It is remarkable to *experience* my own body. To celebrate my own body. To look in the mirror and respond with affirmation, Blessing and thanksgiving. Rejection is so subtle. But LOVE is curious. LOVE will create a path of Blessing. In a woman culture soaked in body jealousies, it is a gentle walk to a higher Beauty Consciousness. It is great Kindness of soul to impart peace to our SISTERS, our mothers, our daughters, ourselves as we struggle to understand,

> RESPECT,
> and LOVE
> our own bodies.

These are certainly *Spiritual* matters:

> Body ESTEEM
> Body INTEGRITY
> Body Aesthetic.
> BODY WISDOM

We neglect them at great cost to our health, creativity and Joy. To realize that I can express GOD in *my* Body is awesome!

What music and laughter do for the heart; dancing and making love do for the body. Prayer is the music of my Soul. Watch me PRAY and you will see my Spirit dancing! But, only if your SPIRIT is dancing too! PRAYER like Dance is self-abandonment.

> unconformed Grace,
> Passion free of instruction,
> LIGHT that swallows darkness,
> Succulent fruit in the first bite,

It IS Experiencing your sparrow-like wings transformed into those of an eagle.

Don't you want to Dance?
Don't You?
Don't you want the Sacred Breath of GOD to flow from the heavenlies through the canyons of the Universe into your *natural* Body?

If you do, then let GO and LET your Body Pray! Allow your body to say that which you do not have language to utter.

The DANCE is IN you.
The Spirit of the Dance is calling to you.
JESUS CHRIST is LORD of the Cosmic Dance.
The first Step—INCARNATION.
Second Step—CRUCIFIXION.
Third Step—RESURRECTION.
Your Step—INVOCATION . . . . .

Call upon His Name.
Welcome Him.
Welcome Him Home to your heart.

Soul and Body are uniquely suited for an exhilarating friendship. The Spirit can heal the Body and the Body can celebrate the Spirit. The call to Dance, is a call to be united in Body and Soul before the LORD. The Glory Dance is within each of us.
The Glory Dance is seeping into our very cells from the fires of PENTECOST.

SEVEN

PRAYER OF A LOST-FOUND DANCER

"GOD, my Delight.
GOD, my Sorrow.
GOD of the unvoiced word.
  the undisclosed horizon.
  the echo of the newborn.
I belong to You.
The laughter in my toes.
The wisdom of my navel.
The memories in the palms of my hands.
I belong to You.
Enjoy YOURSELF,
Make Glory Joy.
Express Divinity.
I belong to You."

Amen.

"My soul longs, indeed it faints for the courts of the LORD; my heart and my flesh sing for joy to the living God."

(Psalms 84:2)

SEVEN

Every Cojourner now knows that
To Pray is
To Believe is
To Pray . . .
This PRAYING breaks the shackles of bondage, infirmity and Dread.
This is TOTAL Prayer. A Dancer's JOY.

Our prayers will not go unheard.
We will no longer be RESTRAINED.
Our Bodies have been *touched* by the SPIRIT and we MUST DANCE.

It's time to dance!
    Unashamed.
    Uncensored.
    Unchoreographed.
    Unrehearsed.

It's time to Dance. (Ecclesiastes 3:4)
If I have to think about it; it's not Prayer. When the focus of my attention is solely the human predicament—mine or someone else's—I am not yet honored by the spirit of prayer. This Holy Dance is a GOD Reality.

    For the Oblate, PRAYER is communion. PRAYER is sight. PRAYER is Wisdom. PRAYER is FIRE. PRAYER is GOD. The very hinges are shaken off the gates of the heavenlies, when we prevail in PRAYER. The incense singes the hair of our nostrils when by PRAYER we enter God's Holy place. And we are welcomed by the Spirit of the LORD. This is the GLORY. The GLORY of GOD. Who can attain unto such Grace?
    The contrite.
    The broken.
    The faithful.
    The Innocent.
    The "obsolete"
    The Mystic.
    The pragmatist.
    The circumcised.
    The Uncircumcised.
    THE FORGIVEN.
    The forgotten.

THE GLORY AND THE DANCE AND THE GLORY • 251

Seven generations of dead-alive witnesses of deliverance from oppression. **SEVEN**
 The voice-less.
 The anonymous.
 Those of eloquent consolations.
 The restless.
 The beautiful.
 The ready-to-obey the Vision of God.
 The solitary Apostle.
 Exiled prophetesses.
 Aborted babies.
 Landless martyrs.
 Crippled dancers.
 Blind musicians.
 Wandering shepherds.
 Three Wise men.
 Any Virgin.
 One Ethiopian eunuch.
 The "last who become first"
 and . . .
 . . . The Midnight Born-Again.

This is the GLORY of the "only begotten of the Father." (John 1:14)

SEVEN

"The glory that you have given me I have given them, so that they may be one, as we are one,"

(John 17:22)

"Moses said, "Show me your glory, I pray."

(Exodus 33:18)

GLORY given to us by the Son
PRIMORDIAL.
Uncreated.
Eternal.
This GLORY cannot be feigned, stolen or appropriated.
This GLORY will not be compromised or negotiated.
This GLORY is in us   (Col. 1:27)
        upon us   (Isa. 60:1)
        Beyond us.   (2 Cor. 3:7–18)

When the Oblate dances, she is PRAYING to live to the "PRAISE of GOD's GLORY." For the GLORY of the LORD is the signature of His Presence. God reigns in the GLORY. God reveals the Kingdom in the GLORY. God demonstrates and confers Power in the GLORY. There is no utterance but God's when the Glory descends. The GLORY of the LORD is an enduring Radiance. A splendor beyond compare. A LIGHT that transfigures. A most excellent shining-forth of the LOVE of God. This LIGHT is a not-visible *visible* Reality. It is discerned by the Oblate while remaining unidentifiable to the unbelieving. For the latter it is the unconfessed NAME—a mere "phenomenon!" But to the heart of faith, it is Beatitude. It is wonder. It is amazing.

    It is Jesus.
    It is Jesus.
    It is Jesus.
    It is undeniably JESUS.

The Dance *and* the GLORY are the signature of GOD.
The Dance *and* the GLORY are the integrity of the Church.
The Dance *and* the GLORY are the future of the Just.
The healing of the nations will be ministered in the Dance and the GLORY.
And so shall world Peace be proclaimed.

THE GLORY AND THE DANCE AND THE GLORY

The GLORY is a transforming Reality. Once embraced by the Light, endued with the LIGHT,
> seized.
> encompassed.
> led.
> protected.
> healed.
> by the Light—

It is no small matter that the Oblate will be changed! Transfiguration is imminent, interior and ultimate. **Imminent**, because "natural" time ceases to be in effect. Expectation is shaped in Hope through Faith. It is an **interior** Reality because the issues of the Spirit impinge upon the heart and the mind. Thirdly, the change is **Ultimate** because it is in flow with the salvific covenant by which we receive Eternal Life.

This GLORY is in symbiosis with the POWER. In other words, although they differ one from the other, each is celebrated in the other. In prevailing PRAYER we experience the POWER *in* the GLORY:

The POWER to withstand and defeat EVIL because the GLORY is a "surpassing" GLORY.

The POWER to heal the Church because the GLORY is unitive.

The POWER to ascend to the throne of GOD because the GLORY sits at the right hand of the Father interceding for us.

A Life of PRAYER is a life lived in the GLORY flow. The Simplicity of such a life is overwhelming to both religionists and the unbelieving.

> **By the POWER of PRAYER, Simplicity can shape your life inwardly and outwardly.**
> **PAUSE to envision a Life of SIMPLICITY. PRAY for the GRACE to desire and to**
> > **LIVE it.**

SEVEN

"but when one turns to the Lord, the veil is removed."
(2 Corinthians 3:16)

"I consider that the sufferings of this present time are not worth comparing with the glory about to be revealed to us."
(Romans 8:18)

SEVEN

Because of the POWER in the GLORY—
I am able to resist the seduction of materialism.
I am enabled to become ego-less in the "competitive"
  system of religion,
I am able to respect my Soul need for
>> Silence.
>> Stillness.
>> Transition.
>> Space.

I am Open to relanguaging my Prayer life.
>> my Presence in the world.
I am able to reshape my behavior.
>> Honor the not-visible.
>> Yield to the supernatural.
>> REST.

BECAUSE of the POWER in the GLORY—
>> LOVE is first in my Life.
>> LOVE is everything in my Life.
>> LOVE is my LIFE.

I know that there is POWER in the GLORY because—
I dance when I "should" be offended.
I dance for the nations.
I dance in the Church.
I dance with GOD.
>> When I Dance, the GLORY reigns.
>>>> the GLORY heals.
>>>> the GLORY shines.
> ALL praises to the GOD of GLORY.
> ALL praises to the GOD of GLORY.

Life in the GLORY, although Simple is comprehensive.